Missouri Shadows

a journey through the lesser known, the famous and the infamous haunts of Missouri

Dan Terry

edited by Glen and Sue Blesi

Cover Photo:
Headlights on Enoch's Knob Bridge over Boeuf Creek in northwestern Franklin County. The "eyes" in the photo were not created with special effects, but are reproduced here from an actual 35 mm photograph.
Photo by Christine Ransom.

ISBN13: 978-0-9797654-0-7
ISBN: 0-9797654-0-4

Missouri Kid Press
P. O. Box 111
Stanton, Missouri 63079

Table of Contents

About the Author

Dan Terry is a Franklin County, Missouri native. He attended school in Stanton and Sullivan, where he participated in public speaking competitions, advancing to state level. He graduated in 1981.

Dan, like many local youths, worked as a guide in Meramec Caverns, where he developed an interest in history.

After a four-year hitch in the United States Coast Guard, he began a career in law enforcement, almost as an accident. In 1995, Terry went to work for the New Haven Police Department, and was promoted to Assistant Chief of Police in 2006. Later that year, he was given the Medal of Honor for pulling a wounded deputy out of the line of fire during a gunfight.

As a child, Dan became fascinated with the paranormal, mostly through such television shows as the Twilight Zone, Night Gallery, and Kolchack: The Night Stalker. After getting a driver's license and a car, he began investigating local haunted places with a small group of friends. During his Coast Guard days, he continued to go to alleged haunted places, using the old 1970's ghost hunting tactics of 'Scare me'.

After concentrating on career and family for many years, Dan was finally able to return to ghost hunting. He visited many haunted places and, with the help of Missouri Paranormal Research members, learned new procedures, such as how to get EVP's and paranormal photography. He is now known as "Spookstalker". Dan has investigated homes and businesses from Wilmington, North Carolina to Cimmeron, New Mexico, including a very haunted museum in Wichita, Kansas, the Crescent Hotel in Eureka Springs, Arkansas, and was one of the early investigators of the Waverly Hills Sanitarium in Louisville, Kentucky.

After writing a newspaper article for the *New Haven Leader* about local haunted spots in 2005, he began writing for *Haunted Times Magazine,* becoming a regular contributor and, in 2007, published his first book, *Beyond the Shadows: Exploring the Ghosts of Franklin County.* He has also been published in police-related magazines.

His published articles include an interview with Lt. Col. Jesse Marcel Jr., the last man acknowledged to have touched the debris from the 1947 Roswell crash, and other articles about Roswell and ghost hunting.

Dan Terry makes his home in New Haven, with his wife Sherri.

—Sue Blesi, Publisher

Foreword

As the editorial director of *Haunted Times* magazine and author of *Searching the Abyss,* I often have the pleasure of working with some of the most recognizable names in the paranormal community such as John Zaffis, Chip Coffey and Christopher Moon.

It is a great position; I can work in the field on investigations or research some of the most famous locations in the world side-by-side with them. Recently, I had a chance to explore the Florida Everglades in search of the Skunk Ape, an interesting trip to say the least. However, meeting new people and working with them in developing content for the magazine is even more rewarding.

Occasionally, a person comes along who has the drive, knowledge and experience to be mentioned alongside the most well known investigators in the community. One person who deserves that same respect is Dan Terry, aka the Spookstalker. I remember working with Dan on his first article for the magazine entitled, Welcome to Hell's Greasy Spoon (*Haunted Times* magazine, Volume2 - Issue 1, 2007); I could tell Dan was different. The article, based on a haunting of a diner on Route 66, jumped off the page and the evidence collected at the site was even better.

At first glance, it was easy to see how the 20-year police veteran was utilizing some of the techniques used in the years of fighting crime to aid him and his team in the investigation of some of the most legendary and haunted sites in the world. In talking with him, I found many similarities in our investigative techniques and beliefs in the paranormal. As a military veteran, I, like Dan, understand the importance of paying attention to the small details a location may be giving you; the small hints to the unknown presence that exist around every corner.

After the success of his first book, *Beyond the Shadows, Exploring the Ghosts of Franklin County,* Dan has continued to supply the readers of *Haunted Times* with some great articles, taking the readers on detailed journeys into the unexplained. He has also done a tremendous job building material for this, his follow-up to his popular and ultra creepy debut effort.

In *Missouri Shadows,* Dan weaves his way through some of the most mysterious and infamous hauntings in the state of Missouri. When I read the book in preparation for this forward, I was captivated. The frightening stories within these pages kept me on the edge of my seat and created a temptation to take a trip to Missouri and investigate them on my own; a trip that I would only take if I could have Dan as my guide.

As I close, I hope all of you enjoy this book as much as I have. The stories inside are full atmosphere, perfect for those brisk windy nights where every sound is magnified by the silence. On those same nights, Dan, like Carl Kolchack the Night Stalker, may be in that wind searching for the answers to the mysterious phenomena that plagues the unseen world, while keeping us safe from the unknown specters that reside in the shadows.

Mark A. Mihalko
Haunted Times Magazine
Editorial Director

Introduction

A young, dynamic, handsome politician from Illinois, who seemed to come out of nowhere, was about to capture the election for U.S. Senator. His friendly demeanor belied his intentions. EVIL!

A reporter became suspicious of his sudden, unstoppable rise from unknown to future Presidential hopeful. His research uncovered the demonic deal made by the unknown politician to exchange his own soul for the chance to lead his nation into the grips of Satan. After attempting to trade the reporter his soul in exchange for a fantastic career in news reporting, the politician tried to silence the reporter by murder. The reporter, Carl Kolchack, had a secret weapon: a small vial of Holy Water.

He destroyed the satanic charm around the neck of the politician, turning him from the evil canine into a small puppy for eternity.
And on that night in November 1974, when The Devil's Platform episode of the Night Stalker series aired for the first time on network television, an eleven-year-old boy sat spellbound. I watched the show and was introduced to a new world, unseen by my parents who were raised in the depression era, pragmatic Baptists who were determined to never again suffer the hunger they had experienced during the depression. Ghosts, demons, vampires, and other such creatures of nightmares were for the foolish.

But their son began a journey that night which continues to this day. I read any book I could find on ghosts, UFOs, Bigfoot, any mystery of the world. I suffered the ridicule of other kids until I learned to keep my interest in the macabre quiet. I began walking through graveyards, old, deserted homes, and other places reported to be ghostly. When I got a driver's license, some friends and I began checking out haunted places, looking for a good scare more than scientific evidence.

After some time in the U.S. Coast Guard, I began a career in law enforcement. A newborn son and adult life kept me from exploring the haunted history of Missouri, but I continued to read. *Haunted Houses* and *More Haunted Houses*, by Richard Winer and Nancy Osborn, really pointed me in the right direction. *The Demonologist,* about Ed and Lorraine Warren, taught me that there was more than Casper-The-Friendly-Ghost waiting out there.

As the kids got older and I became more financially stable, as well as gaining a wife who was even braver than me, I was able to take up ghost hunting again. From Wilmington, North Carolina to Cimarron, New Mexico, I checked out every commercial haunted house and tour available. Eventually, I wrote a newspaper story about haunted places around New Haven, Mo., which was widely accepted. The commercial success of TV's "Ghost Hunters" and the various clones of that show opened the topic for reasonable discussion.

So many people who had experiences but had kept quiet about them were now willing to speak of supernatural happenings.

One person who allowed an experience to change his life was Steven LaChance. After living through a demonic infestation of his house, he fled in fear for the safety of his children. Fueled by finding a lack of competent help for Missourians who were victims of an extreme haunting, LaChance then formed Missouri Paranormal Research.

Eventually teaming up with Greg Meyers, they endeavored to help me as I moved from the ghost-hunting tactics of the 1970s into this century. They taught me better ways to do EVPs which increased my captures tenfold. While Steven has moved on, both he and Greg continue to call me in to assist them with investigations, and I appreciate all their help as well as their confidence in me.

Tim Clifton is another person whose help has been invaluable. I enjoy working with Tim, and I know that if there is a ghost around, he'll find it.

The investigations in this book are real. There are only a few chapters concerning situations I did not personally cover, but instead wrote about other people's experiences. I assure you that when I'm describing a haunting that I investigated, every word is the gospel truth.

Enjoy the book, and fear not. Evil spirits will not be attracted to you because you read the book and, if you do find yourself under psychic attack some day, there are people to help. You'll meet several of them in the following pages.

Happy Hauntings!

Author's Web Site:

Dan Terry www.spookstalker.com

Photo by Carla Strnad

***After discussing the religious aspects of ghost hunting** with her family, Carla Strnad went to her church to pray for guidance. She photographed the interior of the church and was amazed to discover an orb on the right side of Jesus as he hung on the cross and a huge, brightly glowing orb in the right hand of Jesus on a portrait. This helped Carla deal with her doubts.*

How to Ghost Hunt
no experience needed

In writing this, I think about a statement I heard one night from a guest on Coast to Coast AM with Art Bell, a paranormal radio show that airs every night at midnight here in Missouri. The guest made a comment which I will paraphrase: Beware of anyone who calls himself an expert on ghosts; he's out to get your money.

The more I thought about that statement, the more sense it made. We can't reproduce paranormal situations in a lab. We can't guess where or when they will occur, so how could anyone be an expert? Some people have a lot more experience in it than others. John Zaffis, for example, has been involved with paranormal research for some thirty years. Lorraine Warren, a professional demonologist, has likely been at it nearly 50 years. Hans Holzer probably has been doing it for even longer!

But expert? Be careful of anyone who claims such a title.

That said, I want to add a chapter for those who want to ghost hunt. Some so-called professional ghost hunters will disagree on much of what I say. I can only pass on the lessons I have learned.

<u>Definitions</u>

As you read this book and learn about ghost hunting in general, you'll come across some of the following terms. This is not all of the ghost-hunting vocabulary you will find, and definitions often change from hunter to hunter, but these short explanations should help you on your journey.

- Anomaly: Something on a photo, video, or recorder that has no logical explanation.
- Apparition: A spirit in human or animal form. Very rare. This is what we're all looking for.
- Casper: This is a term I use for happy, friendly, even playful ghosts.
- Demon: Evil spirit—has never been human. Demons are angels that were thrown out of Heaven when Satan rebelled, and they have what can only be called a psychopathic hate for humans.
- Dowsing rods: Thin metal rods, usually copper, used to communicate with spirits. The same type of rod is used to find water.

- Ectoplasm: An overused term for fog, smoke or a milky substance often seen in photos.
- EMF meter: A device used to locate and measure electromagnetic fields. It is widely believed that spirits are made up of electromagnetic energy.
- EVP: Electronic Voice Phenomenon, or voices recorded but not heard until later.
- Intelligent Haunting: Ghosts who interact with the family or investigators. They can make their presence known by moving things or answering questions by sound.
- Orbs: One of the most disputed supernatural phenomena, orbs are balls of light captured by photos that could be spirit energy, souls, or dust or moisture. I have also seen orbs that were green, blue and white.
- Residual haunting: Not an intelligent haunting, this is just energy with no focus. What you see or hear is a simple replay of earlier events. They are not aware of your presence at all. Compare it to putting a VCR on "play" and leaving the room. The sound and images are there, but they have no idea whether you are there or not.
- Shadow people: One of the biggest mysteries in ghost hunting. Black figures of humans or animals that seem to watch us, but usually flee quickly if seen by humans. Ghosts that can't become apparitions, or something else?
- Sprites: Small flashes of light in a dark room. I believe this is a sign that the ghosts are nearby.
- Vortex: An opening to the other side.

<u>The Hunt</u>
Don't get complicated!

If you find a haunted location that is active, you'll probably encounter one or more of these four types of hauntings.

1. Residual: This is not a real ghost, but a playback like a VCR recording. It has no thought, no knowledge of your presence.
2. Intelligent: Real ghosts that can either ignore or interact with you in which case you'll get knockings or EVP's in response to your requests or questions.

3. Demonic: Not so much hauntings although they often pretend to be so—more like an infestation of evil in the area. To quote a demon from a famous movie, 'GET OUT!'
4. Shadow people: No explanation for them, they are just there. While they seem to be harmless, the demonic often pretend to be shadow people or Caspers to gain your trust.

Try to check out the place ahead of time. Don't trespass, and take ID in case the police are called. Check the history of the site. I can't begin to relate the hours I've spent in front of a screen looking at old newspapers on microfilm, searching for the issue relating to a murder or accident. This part is tedious, but when you call to the spirit by his name, you tend to get more of a reaction.

I've seen groups go into a small haunted home with ten or more people. I've found that a ghost-hunting group consisting of two to four people is enough unless the investigation involves a huge place like the Waverly Hills Hospital or a battleship. Sometimes, four is too many. I've also seen groups bring in people that only think or say they want to be ghost hunters and the situation quickly devolves into a gossip session, or people who are afraid to be there and won't stop talking. You can't hear the spirits' attempts to communicate if you're talking. Yet, some insist on telling their war stories from other haunts or just yacking to hear their heads rattle. Keep your team small.

That said, another useful tool I've found is to ignore the ghost, carrying on your own conversation about something else and making it angry or jealous. But this is a tool. Be careful not to get so wrapped up in your own storytelling that you miss what's going on around you.

Another bit of advice is don't go cheap! When I started trying to do it the scientific way instead of the old 70's 'scare me' investigation, I used a micro tape recorder, a three mega-pixel camera and an $11 EMF detector. That just whetted my whistle for the investigation and showed me just how much evidence I was missing.

Suddenly, I had to have a seven mega-pixel camera, a $60 K2 meter, and a digital recorder with the ability to download the sound into the computer. Since then, I've picked up another recorder, and a digital video recorder with nightshot at $500. Some go on to purchase DVR systems with computers and video cameras that can go down several hallways. Now, I'm after a 12 mega-pixel camera with SLR that takes photos as fast as a 35mm camera. When you start out cheap, you'll get angry with yourself the first time you see something, but can't get a clear photo because the camera was just too small, or the recorder won't download into a computer.

Always bring spare batteries. Mine are known to have suddenly drained, and having to go for more can really mess up the whole hunt. I've recently seen people take crank flashlights. Remember, you'll make enemies when, right in the middle of an EVP, the rrrrrrrrrrrrrrrrrrrr sound of some cheapskate cranking his flashlight covers whatever was being said by the ghostly speaker. Use batteries.

<u>On The Scene</u>

Once you're at the suspected haunting site, divide up into your teams and decide what equipment is going where. Again, two teams of two each are optimum for me. If you're investigating for someone, they should take you to the areas of the most activity. Remember, ghosts are not bound by our limitations. They can travel anywhere in the house unseen but remember to watch for movement from the corner of your eye. You'll catch it more often that way because that part of your eye is more sensitive. Don't worry if you don't see what others do; in this case, practice does make perfect. Other than a shadow person I saw at Boondockers in New Haven, it took two years for me to see them regularly. Now, I see them almost everywhere.

Some like to take this time to ask for prayers of protection. It's probably a good idea if you suspect demonic activity. Others, though, believe that it may drive the spirits away, which is counter productive if you're ghost hunting. I usually hold the prayers for protection until I leave, again, unless it's suspected to be evil.

Refrain from unnecessary talking during the EVP session. One person should ask the questions, or have someone else start. After working with someone for a while, you'll be able to change without signals. Many times, it's better to let the women do it, or just the men, depending on the spirit. Also, while attempting EVP's, remember to give the spirits time to build up the energy and answer. Give several seconds between each question, or you won't know which question they are answering.

If I am in someone's home, or someplace such as Boondockers where I knew the business owners were happy with the ghosts, I don't challenge them strongly. In other places, insults and threats work when trying to get a spirit to communicate. However, if there is evil about, this can bring problems down on you. Be careful when you start with the threats and insults.

Listen to your body. Once, while sitting in a basement, I felt a tingle on the back of my neck, and called for someone to take a photo. At that exact moment, one of the team members took a photo and I asked her to check it. There was a basketball-size orb behind my head.

While taking EVP's, remember not to whisper. It may come across as mysterious mumbling or talking. Speak in a low, but clear voice, so others can recognize it.

I've been on two investigations involving children. In one, a group had already checked it out and found nothing. The mother still believed there might be something evil around, and asked me to try. I spent several hours with the child, taking some 300 photos. The child played and talked, as kids do, telling me the stories which all involved a new movie bad guy. Then, as if it were a second thought, he just mentioned, "There is a ghost in that corner." He never looked up. I had been trying to get him to tell me about the shadow people at his grandmother's house and when I asked about that, he said "No, in that corner there," pointing to the corner in his room, adding, "It's still there."

My wife, Sherri, took photos and we got the only orbs of the entire room right there. The kid could see the ghost and wasn't at all afraid.

In another case, a child was having almost identical experiences. A DVR system was set up, and we uncovered some of the most interesting orb activity I have ever seen. At one point, an orb entered through a closed window, stopped inches from a cat's face, then leaped up and circled the room before leaving through another closed window. A few moments later, another orb came from behind the couch, circled the child and left, with the family dog following its trajectory with his head. That case turned into my first demonic case. I called in Steven LaChance to assist, along with Tim Clifton and Theresa Reavy, and it turned into a fight with the evil force being chased back to the basement, then escaping and going upstairs where it began making a ruckus, throwing things around the kid's room. Steven went back upstairs and began the prayer attack again, eventually driving the force outside.

It never hurts to have someone on call to help if you get in over your head.

As you go through this book, you will notice there are no haunted cemeteries. Some argue that cemeteries are not haunted, because nothing ever happens there. People seldom die in a graveyard. That would be way too convenient. Others believe cemeteries can be haunted. I've even heard the idea that Christians are waiting beside their bodies for the last trump!

Cemeteries are often haunted. I don't know why, but recently I was at a supposedly-haunted graveyard in the daytime, and one photo Sherri took showed what appeared to be a robed and hooded figure watching me from the tree line.

I decided not to write about the haunted boneyards because, unfortunately, some misguided people go to them for a good scare and decide to tear them up. While writing this book, three cemeteries in a nearby town were damaged, with over 100 stones turned over and broken by vandals. At least two of the creepy criminals were found and charged. I don't want to be responsible for such damage. If you decide to hunt in a graveyard, show some respect for the deceased. You'll be joining them eventually.

Another thing I discovered concerns wearing black. It seems people believe they are required to wear black clothing while on a ghost hunt. Some investigators can pull this off. Once at a night conference I met a guy wearing a black trench coat and mirror sunglasses. He had long graying hair and looked like a forty-year-old extra from "The Matrix". I wouldn't let someone dressed like that hunt for roaches in my house, let alone ghosts.

One night, during a training investigation on the Enoch's Knob Bridge, I got a photo of what appeared to be a glowing face hovering behind an investigator. Once we got it on the computer and blown up, we could see it was another investigator, her face reflecting the light from the back of her camera and her black shirt hiding the rest of her body from view. Now, I wear light-colored shirts to avoid such problems.

Most people discover that they are good at some things and not others. Find your niche but don't ignore the other parts. Jamie Eckerle, co-founder of Missouri State Paranormal Investigators, gets a lot of great EVP's. Tom Halstead, a lead investigator for the Paranormal Task Force, gets awesome photos. Tim Clifton gets psychic flashes, and there is a ghost around if he says so. Possibly due to my police experience, I detect the movement of shadow people and any movement in darkness.

I get a few EVP's, and a few good photos and still carry the K2 meter and thermometer. Concentrate on your skill, but don't give up the other evidence.

One of the most frustrating things I see from other investigators is the desire to leave just as things are getting interesting. You're there to find evidence of ghosts. You may get touched, things may get thrown, or you may see a shadow moving towards you, or hear a voice. Now is not the time to leave.

If you feel you just have to leave, do so in an orderly fashion. I would estimate that 90 percent of the injuries that occur because of ghosts are caused by the fear of the investigators, not by a spirit.

Once I worked with a group that was very anal about evidence. The lead investigator had so many rules for gathering evidence, and not contaminating it, that the hunt was no fun.

It is unlikely that anyone reading this will get earth-shattering evidence that the paranormal exists and, as a result, be able to change the minds of the world. If you get a video of a horned, red-skinned Satan with a pointed tail and forked tongue spitting fire, someone will scream "Photoshop" and most people will back him. Don't let it get to you, and enjoy the hunt. You'll never get to 'bag' a ghost and mount the head above the fireplace with crossed EMF detectors underneath to brag to your friends about. You will have your stories to tell on dark, stormy nights or around the campfire, hopefully with a decent photo or EVP for evidence. It's enough.

A group in Kansas was allowed into a very haunted home for an investigation. They rearranged the furniture for their own use, leaving it and the mess right where it was. That family was so upset that no team has been allowed in since.

Remember to be polite to the hosts, and professional to the ghosts. Word of mouth has gotten me a lot of investigations and I have worked hard to maintain a good reputation.

I recently heard of a family having paranormal problems. They called for assistance from a "Paranormal Expert". The victim reported that the people came in, did a psychic and scientific-looking investigation, and charged $400. When the haunting continued, they informed her that an angry demon was attached to one of the antiques she collected, and for a mere $300 they would take her antique collection and bury it in a cemetery so it would be in Holy Ground. The victim later called into a radio show to ask if she had made a mistake.

I don't know of any paranormal group that charges a fee. Don't be fooled by fake psychics and Ghostbuster-style equipment. You can shop for an investigator the same way you would for a dentist.

One thing the paranormal investigator will hear is that seeking the spirits is an affront to God. Many believe that there is a passage in the Bible forbidding mortals from investigating spiritual activity. Many others believe that orbs or spirits seen by humans are all evil, as human souls go immediately to judgment upon death.

I won't attempt to change the mind of any religious folks. It is impossible to force change or argue religion with any positive result. I have asked people to show me these passages and have not seen one yet.

Carla Strnad, whom I met during book signings, came across the same argument with her family. Carla discovered she can ask for orbs, or for the spirits to show themselves, and they seem almost to pose at her request.

After a confusing discussion with her family about the religious aspects of ghost hunting, she went to her church and prayed for guidance. Carla then photographed the interior of the church, and in one photo there was an orb on the right side of Jesus as he hung on the cross and a huge, brightly glowing orb in the right hand of Jesus on a portrait! This helped Carla deal with the doubts.

Ghost hunting has been an exciting adventure for me. I've met some fantastic people, and made some really good friends. I've also met a few kooks. Start with a few ghost tours. Try an overnight with Troy Taylor, or at the McPike Mansion in Alton, IL, and see if you enjoy it. Pay attention to your feelings, and take others' feelings with a grain of salt. After you see a shadow person run away, or hear your first EVP and you were there, you'll understand why we do this.

"It is required of every man," the ghost returned, "that the spirit within him should walk abroad among his fellow-men, and travel far and wide; and, if that spirit goes not forth in life, it is condemned to do so after death."

—Charles Dickens

Photo by Dan Terry

***The Sweet Memories Antique Shop and Ice Cream Parlor** in Potosi offers hospitality to guests; some invited, some less welcome. It would be best to keep any remarks about not believing in ghosts to yourself until you are clear of the building. The house dates back to 1869 and has been the site of at least one death.*

Washington County, Missouri

Chapter 1

Lady of the House

a former resident is more than a sweet memory

Potosi, Missouri was founded in 1799 to serve the lead mining community that had sprung up in the area. Founded by Moses Austin, it was named for a silver mining town in Bolivia. Potosi means "noisy place" in a South American Indian tongue.

In 1813, Washington County, Missouri, was founded, with Potosi as the county seat, after Moses Austin donated 40 acres of land for the new town. Moses Austin became known for more than the founding of Washington County. In 1821, after a trip to Texas, Austin received permission to form a colony there. He died later that year, but his son, Stephen Austin, led 300 families from Washington County to Texas, and became known as the Father of Texas. The Texas capital of Austin was named for him, making Moses Austin the Grandfather of Texas.

A drive down Highway 8 reveals the struggle of the small town to survive in an era when local mines are closing down. A state prison was built nearby, providing much-needed jobs to the area.

One block off Highway 8, at 105 W. Breton Street is a two-story home built in the 1800s. A large sign outside designates the business as "Sweet Memories" and a second line proclaims, "sandwich shop, ice cream and antiques."

Looking at the outside of the small home, which has been converted to a business, no one would believe it is haunted. But there is no doubt in the mind of the owner, Cindy Merx. Cindy, who has operated a catering and baking business there for the past six years, loves to talk of the spirit and has allowed several paranormal groups to visit. But the most fun she's had was with her own employees.

"In the kitchen, the cabinets didn't always have doors. Instead, they had a lip that prevented things from falling out." Cindy explained, "One day, I was telling one of my newer employees, a young man, very serious, who said 'Well, I don't believe in ghosts.' Then a large can of mandarin oranges lifted up over the lip and fell at his feet!"

"The ghost could have hit him with the can, and hurt him. She is harmless, but does not like to be told she don't exist."

Cindy sounds proud of her ghost. "It's never scary, but sometimes it's irritating." She related things missing, moved and thrown. "Once, one of my employees and I saw a noodle, one noodle, thrown from the empty kitchen and landed at our feet." Harriett just wanted them to know she was there.

In 1869, the house was purchased by Garrett Van Allen, who was one of the first prosecuting attorneys of Washington County. He moved to the house from Albany, N. Y., with his wife and several children. In 1871, his first wife, Harriet, died in the house at the age of 44. In 1880, Garrett remarried—this time to a woman named Mary. Garrett died in 1899 at age 75.

The house then went to Francis Hoeman, then to Francis Connolly. Al and Joyce Weiss lived there for nearly a half of a century. David and Cindy Merx are the present owners.

One day, a lady came into the sandwich shop and told Cindy she used to live in the house. After beating around the bush, she finally asked Cindy if she had met Sarah. Cindy asked who Sarah was, and the woman said it was a name her family had given the ghost who occupied the house. Cindy then gently corrected her, saying, "Her name is Harriett."

Cindy only assumes the ghost is Harriett, as Harriett is the only woman known to have died in the house. One thing she does know is that the spirit does not like non-believers. And she plays games.

On the day I arrived, the sleigh bells rang loudly as I opened the door and walked inside. Finding no one, I assumed it was closed and left.

Cindy caught up with me before I got back into the car. Later, she explained that Harriett likes to open and close the door, to the point that most folks around Potosi know to yell out if they enter the business, because Cindy and her employees seldom check the door when they hear it.

"I send people into the storeroom to get something, and it's been moved. One of my people saw a white mist inside the storeroom, and once, when two of my sisters, an employee, and myself were standing in the kitchen and one sister said she don't believe in ghosts, a cutting board, which is kept behind the faucet on the sink, lifted up and fell into the sink with a loud thunk. She's a believer now."

Cindy didn't know it was haunted when she bought it. But the spirit made her presence known: a puzzle was finished for her, the creamer taken out of the small metal tub and the tub hidden, only to be found a few days later on a counter. Cindy and another employee once saw a shadow of a small child run across the room. But, there was no child present—at least not a living one.

MPR has been among the many ghost-hunting groups that have been allowed to investigate. Cindy related that Steven LaChance and Theresa Reavey both felt the presence and several group members refused to go either upstairs or into the basement. This has occurred with most of the teams.

But Cindy is not afraid of either place. "Once, an employee whom I had baked a pie for, came up to get it before I got to work. She called me, screaming. She had picked up the pie, gone outside and, when she turned to lock the door, she saw a ghostly woman standing on the stairway beyond the door, just looking at her."

Once, when she had decorated the bathroom for Halloween, including making a bathtub up to look like a coffin, someone came in and asked to see it. Cindy had finished the room less than 10 minutes before.

The customer asked her how she could make that door open so slowly as she approached, and with the long sssqqqqeeeeeeeeeeekkkkk, like a cheap horror movie. Cindy didn't tell her that the door was not rigged up like that, that the ghost was helping. After Halloween, the ghost was not ready to quit her game; Cindy was forced to fix the annoying squeak with a can of WD-40.

One employee placed a tablecloth on a table. Moments later, she returned to the room to find it on the floor. Once again, she put it on the table. Again, it was removed and thrown on the floor. This time, she put it in a wad on top of the table, and again it was thrown off. She complained to Cindy, who gave her a simple reason. Harriett didn't like that one!

A trip to Potosi would not be complete without a stop at Sweet Memories. Have an ice cream and some stories from Cindy. Just wait until you are outside to say you don't believe in ghosts. Harriett finds that quite rude.

Lady of the House

This is easy. Little Old Lady ghost, probably hanging around 'cause she thinks she left the iron on.

—Angel, Season I, Room With a View

Photo by Dan Terry

The Parlor Bed and Breakfast at Ironton, *completed in 1908, was once a private residence and later served as a funeral parlor. It was opened as a bed and breakfast in 2000 after an extensive restoration. Owner Jeanette Schrum reports that the spirits began manifesting themselves while the building was being readied for its new life.*

Iron County, Missouri

Chapter 2

Ghosts of the Valley

a vacation destination for the haunt hunter

The Arcadia Valley lies nestled between mountain tops 80 miles south of St. Louis in the highest part of the Missouri Ozarks. With three small towns bunched together in the heart of the valley, it is as rich in history as the ground is rich in heavy metals.

Coming from St. Louis, the first town in the valley within Iron County is Pilot Knob. In September 1864, a battle took place in this quiet mining valley, driving one of the final nails in the coffin of the Confederacy.

In Virginia, Grant and Lee continued to scuffle over Richmond. General Sherman was marching toward Atlanta, and the Southern cause was on the run. In a last-ditch effort to get Missouri

Photo by Dan Terry

***This depression in the ground near Pilot Knob** was caused by the explosion of a magazine during the Battle of Pilot Knob, a reminder that countless men lost their lives in Civil War battles that were fought in Missouri. Have the soldiers all left or have some stayed near the scene of their last battle?*

into the Confederacy, former governor Gen. Sterling Price had been tasked with taking St. Louis and the state capital, Jefferson City, before the fall elections in the hope of establishing a pro-South government.

On September 9, 1864, a 12,000-man force crossed from Arkansas into Missouri. Among them were blooded units from Texas, units scavenged from other commands, recaptured deserters and conscripts taken by force from farms and villages. Most were clothed in rags and carried water in jugs slung from their shoulders and paper cartridges in the pockets of their frayed coats. Many were barefoot, without tents, blankets, or even guns.

General Shelby wanted to go directly to St. Louis before the Union forces could fortify the city. Price was told to bypass the small garrison at Pilot Knob and continue to the larger prize on the Mississippi.

But, because he needed supplies for his starved, unarmed troops, Price allowed himself to be talked into attacking the Federal garrison at Pilot Knob, known as Ft. Davidson. There, Price believed he would find food, supplies and weapons to prepare his troops for the fight in St. Louis.

Price made another tactical mistake. Instead of following his original plan, which included bombarding the fort with heavy artillery from the top of a nearby mountain, the general decided that the small 1000-man garrison would not be able to stand against his force of over 10,000 men, and elected to attack.

Gen. Ewing, along with portions of the 3rd Missouri State Militia and the 14th Iowa Infantry, prepared for battle. After a few small skirmishes with patrols from both sides, including a battle at the county courthouse in nearby Ironton, the playing field was set with the Union forces in the fort and two rifle trenches, and the Confederate troops on the mountain and across the creek. Nightfall and the onset of heavy rain pushed off the attack until morning.

At dawn on September 27, the fight began with the small patrol in Ironton being forced back to the fort. The first skirmish took place between dismounted Rebel cavalry facing fortified riflemen and Federal artillery. The result was over 200 dead Confederates, but the Union fort was surrounded.

An hour of silence. The calm before the storm. The Rebel army formed into brigades, while the cannons inside the fort were readied with grape shot, or canisters of hundreds of half-inch lead balls to be fired from the cannon like shotgun shot. Riflemen inside the fort took positions along the wall, while others prepared to pass up freshly-loaded rifles as the marksmen fired.

At 2:00 P.M. all hell broke loose.

Confederate artillery began firing. Troop columns moved across the open field toward the fort. Inside the earthen walls, in an echo of the 1814 Battle of New Orleans, the riflemen were told to hold their fire until the enemy was close.

Union artillery opened up on the lines, using the grape shot. Each round fired resulted in multiple hits, as the shot combined with the closeness of the enemy troops made missing impossible. Still, the Confederate officers pushed the troops on. Clouds of smoke blanketed the fort and surrounding valley.

As the soldiers continued to advance, Union soldiers began firing from the rifle pits. Soon, they too were forced back to the relative safety of the fort. The 300 riflemen there, aided by the men reloading for them after each shot using multiple rifles, spewed forth lead like rain.

At 200 yards, with the screams of hundreds of Rebel yells, the Confederate line charged. Union sharpshooters could see only legs through the dense white smoke. At 30 yards, the first group was decimated and fell back.

Lines were reformed quickly and the Confederates attacked again. Again, they were driven back by the incredible amount of shot pouring forth. On the third charge, Rebel troops made it into the dry moat at the foot of the walls. Inside, hand grenades, hastily made from artillery shells, were lobbed into the pit driving the Grey army from the moat before they could scale the walls.

Finally, a retreat was called. For 500 yards, the ground was covered with the dead and dying. Less than an hour had passed, and one of the bloodiest clashes in Civil War history was over.

Another dark, rainy night. General Ewing made the decision to attempt a dangerous retreat. At midnight, with the wheels of the artillery covered for silence, the troops quietly used a rifle trench to escape the fort. In the rain and darkness, with the shock and awe of the great battle still ringing in their ears, Confederate sentries mistook the sounds for their own men moving in the shadows.

Inside the fort, the Union dead were placed against the powder magazine, which was partially buried in the dirt in the center of the fort. At 2:00 A.M., the last troops set explosives and blew up the magazine. It left a crater several yards deep, and the explosion was felt 20 miles away. The Union bodies, which had been placed there in the hope that the resulting dirt storm would bury them, were blown apart. Confederates believed an accident had occurred inside the fort. The next day the truth was discovered and Price was denied his prize.

The troops were re-formed and, due to the damage to his numbers, Price decided against attempting to take St. Louis, marching instead, toward Jefferson City. He left a unit to bury the dead. They placed more than 1000 Confederate soldiers and what Union body parts they could find into a mass grave using one of the rifle pits. Price's army was finished as a fighting force. They engaged in one more small battle at Jefferson City, but the town had been reinforced while Price was wasting time and resources in Iron County. He fought his last real battle at Westport. The war in Missouri was over. Arcadia Valley would return to a mining area.

Where Valor and Devotion Met
North and South
Sept. 26 and 27, 1864

So reads the stone placed to mark the rifle pit where the troops were buried in a mass grave. The area, the state and, eventually, the nation, would get back to business as usual. The scars of the battle would heal, and a state historic park was established at the battle site.

But, can men rest easily after such a battle?

Sherri and I spent several hours at the battlefield on three consecutive nights. I pulled some tricks out of the bag to get the spirits active, including wearing Confederate flags, singing Dixie, and badmouthing the officers who caused the needless bloodbath. We got several interesting photos, including one of a large orb walking along the wall next to me as I investigated. One last sentry, standing his eternal post?

There were also photos of multi-colored orbs near the entrance to the fort. It seems that here, unlike the Antietam or Gettysburg battlefields, the spirits of these brave men rest easily. As inscribed on the stone placed near the mass grave,

> *"...The effort was costly for the Confederate forces, however, and hundreds of them lie buried here, known only to God. They made the supreme sacrifice for the principles in which they believed. A few Union soldiers are interred here also. Whatever transgressions existed on either side, let the passage of time bury amid the ruins of the past; But whatever was noble and honorable, it is our sacred duty to transmit to succeeding generations."*

Rest Inn Peace

In Ironton, the "Parlor" is a bed and breakfast which advertises that it once was a funeral parlor. And, it's haunted.

"I'm not a believer," said Jeannette Schrum, owner and operator of the Parlor. "At least, I wasn't a believer before I started this place. Now, well, I don't know. But there is something here."

Construction was started in 1901. The owner and architect, Charles J. Tual, built it to impress his bride who was from a rich mining family. The concrete blocks were made on site, and after being placed, fire bricks were made and placed next to them, making the walls some 14- to 16-inches thick.

The building was finally finished in 1908, complete with the turret, or round section, where the bricks, windowsills, glass and all woodwork are curved to form the round contours of the structure.

With radiant heat in the rooms, it became one of the most modern homes in the Arcadia Valley. When his bride passed away, Tual lived in the house alone for 20 years, later marrying a girl locals described as a 'party girl'. After Tual's death, the house had several owners, and the talk of it being haunted began early, possibly in the 30's.

During the Depression, Jeannette's grandmother, who was raising Jeannette and her sister, Dana, worked there as a maid two days a week. Jeannette said that while her grandmother, whom she fondly refers to as "Mom", and the owner's wife were good friends, the proprieties were observed at all times.

"Mom couldn't use the front door, but had to go into the house via the back door," said Jeannette. "And she couldn't use the main stairway, but had to use the servants' stairs in the back. And she couldn't use the indoor plumbing, but had to go use the outhouse. But she didn't mind. That's just the way it was back then."

Jeannette believes that one of the spirits in the house is her grandmother, being attached to her rather than the house. "When one group came through, they used dowsing rods. They gave us the rods while they checked out the rest of the house, and my sister and I, along with her husband, tried it out. When the rods started crossing in answer, we asked if it was Mom. The rods indicated the answer was yes.

As a test, I said, 'Mom, your favorite color is yellow.' and they started shaking back and forth crazy. That was Mom! Mom never did put up with our foolishness. Then I said, 'You're right, Mom. Your favorite color is blue.' Then the rods stopped."

But Mom wasn't done. "I asked Mom if she ever thought we'd own this house, and the rods showed no!"

The parlor was opened as a bed and breakfast in August of 2000. Their encounters with the spirits began during the restoration stage. One of the owners assisting with the restoration used to hear someone ask "Hi, how ya doin?" each day. Yet each time he turned around, no one was present. At least no one visible. It always occurred upstairs, and no one could have come up or down that fast.

Robert Halker didn't believe until one day when he was sitting down to read the paper. Jeannette related, "Bob suddenly said 'Oh, damn!' He always says that when he forgets something, so I asked what he forgot. He told me to never mind. When I pressed the issue, he looked up from the paper and said, 'I saw her. She just walked across the room, then stopped and looked right at me.' "

Jeannette and Robert are working on returning the building to its original state. The spirits seem happy with that. Jeannette has some memory of the original appearance as her own great-grandfather's funeral was held there.

In 1960, the home was purchased by Mr. Howell, who already owned one funeral home in the area. At first, he attempted to do the embalming in the basement, but the facilities were not adequate. Howell then attempted to use the facilities from his first home, then transport the body over. According to Jeannette, he only embalmed a couple of bodies there, and had less than two dozen funerals before selling both houses and retiring.

The biggest problems Jeannette has are with the doorbells and clocks. "There is no clock in the house that reads the same time." she said. "The one upstairs has been known to stop for days, then start again and be right!!" That one convinced her sister the place was haunted.

During an all-woman murder mystery held there, an attic door in the Brass Bedroom swung open violently. That room features a large brass bed. In the Waterfall Room, a guest suddenly left in the middle of the night when she watched a water bottle walk across the table and fall to the floor. Jeannette said at first she thought it just slid on the water that had been condensing onto the surface until she went up and looked at it. It slid across a wicker table.

On the evening of the interview, the front doorbell rang while Jeannette, Sherri and I were all in the living room, alone in the building. Jeannette smiled and said I could check, but there would be no one there. Minutes later, the doorbell rang in the back. Again, she said there would be no one there. Jeannette said, "Listen. The dogs in the backyard aren't barking. No one is there." Later, the chimes in the clock upstairs went off at 8:43 P.M. Again, Jeannette smiled. The ghosts love to play.

"When this place is empty," Jeannette told us, "It feels like a museum in here, but when the ghosts are around, it's more like a home."

The Parlor does have a homey feel to it. A lot of it comes from the glowing personality of Jeannette. Ask her about the ghosts, and she'll fill the evening with her stories. Ask about Christmas time at the Parlor.

"One year," Jeannette said, "We had three ornaments here that were battery operated—a mailbox, a Santa Claus, and a snowman. The snowman had to have his foot squeezed to work; the other two were motion activated.

"One couple came in and went upstairs. Suddenly, Santa said, 'Ho, Ho, Ho'. Then the mailbox said, 'You've got Christmas Mail!' Finally, the snowman said, 'Christmas is such a kick!' It continued all night long. And the couple was Jewish! They never came back."

Finally, the snowman was placed in the basement, and the batteries were taken out of the other two. Jeannette said it was too much trouble to get to the batteries in the snowman.

For the rest of the season, she could hear the snowman, which had to be squeezed to operate, yelling its joyful Christmas cheer to the empty basement. This year, none of the decorations had batteries placed in them.

Other than some bright orbs in photos, especially one taken while Sherri was still interviewing Jeannette, and the doorbell games, which continued throughout our entire three-day stay, the best evidence was on the last night, when we were the only guests.

Starting around 1:00 A.M., things were being moved in the room. I could hear the shuffling of objects on the dresser, desk and tables. When I arose, all would stop. Less than a minute after lying back down, it would start again. It seemed that the ghosts knew what we were there for, and wanted to put on a show. I finally just went to sleep. Let the ghosts play.

Looking through the guest comment books, I found several remarks relating to the ghosts:

> *July 6, 2002 . . . p.s. I believe one of the ghosts paid us a visit last night. All of a sudden, I felt a cold chill and the attic door blew open. Now we know it's hot up there, and the AC wasn't running at the time. What or who was it?* CC
> *August 16, 2003 . . . Your lovely and good-natured spirits are what made this inn extra special.* R & M
> *February 15, 2003 . . . for those who follow us, if you open the closet in the Franklin bath, have the complimentary can of ghost repellent handy!* W
> *January 19, 2006 . . . I would say your place is haunted, in my opinion . . . It was a fun sort of scary.* KW

There was more. For those interested, I cannot recommend the Parlor Bed and Breakfast enough. For the beginner, the spirits are happy show-offs. For the family member being dragged along, the breakfast was incredible! Ask Bob for his French toast. I would almost believe the ghosts stay on for the food!

School for Terror

Sitting on 17 acres and surrounded by evergreens and tall oaks, the former Arcadia Academy was founded by Rev. J. C. Berryman in 1846. Originally a Methodist High School, it was quite successful until the Civil War disrupted life throughout the area. The school was turned into a hospital, bringing along with it the horrors of war: death, suffering, the pain of loss and agonized screams of men having limbs removed without the benefit of an anesthetic.

In 1877, the building was purchased by the Ursuline nuns for use as a girls' school. Young ladies were brought in for training from all over the world, including many South American countries.

The girls lived and learned under a strict guideline set down by the nuns, including the observation of silence at all times except during recreation. The school prospered, sometimes educating as many as 100 girls in a year. The education was considered top rate, as was the library and the music department.

In 1970, the last class graduated, and the Arcadia Academy of Ursuline Sisters for Girls became a convent for nuns.

In 1985, the nuns moved to St. Louis, and the academy was sold to private individuals and placed on the National Register of Historic Places as a historic district.

Today, the beautiful old architecture includes a German-designed gym roof and some of the most intricate, detailed stained glass windows in the world. The compound holds two bed-and-breakfast businesses and two antique stores.

But, while the kids, soldiers, and nuns have moved on, there is a remaining host of spiritual residents that seem to let their presence be known.

Working with reporters from the *St. Francois County Daily Journal,* who were looking for a good ghost story for the 2006 Halloween edition, Missouri Paranormal Research investigated the famous Arcadia Academy. Ghost stories had been flying around like the spirits themselves from the old buildings, with the story of a ghostly Confederate soldier even being written about by a previous student. Sue Schlosser Tippitt wrote about this Rebel ghost in her book, *Boarding School Diary,* published by Fortune's Cap Publications in 2005.

While Sherri and I were staying at the Parlor, another couple was staying there after coming into town to pick up a parent, moving him from a Missouri nursing home to one in Colorado.

One of the spouses, who wishes to remain anonymous, said that the first night they came into town, they stopped at one of the B and B's in the Arcadia Academy. After checking the rooms, she privately told her husband that she would rather stay in the car than stay there. She told Sherri and I that there was a feeling of malevolence in the building, and she also felt as if she were being watched. They then went to the Parlor, where they were quite happy.

Most of the MPR team stayed in an area known as the "Priests House." After a particularly nasty demonic haunting in another town, this was billed to the team as a recreational Casper hunt. Theresa Reavey, psychic investigator for MPR, reported several people saw someone standing in the window of a locked room, where no one should have been. During an early walkthrough, a child of one of the investigators came to Theresa, saying he saw a ghostly man in the hallway. The young child described the spirit as wearing all black, with a small white spot under his chin. This would describe the reported spirit priest, whom other investigators had also heard giving a sermon to an invisible congregation.

Investigator Tim Clifton, as he walked through the hallway checking out the interior of the building, reported the doorknob on one of the bedroom doors was rattling. Knowing it was Theresa Reavey's room, Tim called out "Theresa"! Suddenly, the doorknob turned completely, and the door opened by itself, revealing a room empty of living inhabitants.

Later, another investigator told Reavey that he saw her door slam open, even though she was not in the area. While he saw no one in her room, he did report to her the odor of sulfur, so strong it made him gag. Reavey said they checked the door, which was solid oak. When it was shut, no one on the team could force it open.

In a room called the "Bishops room", the spirit of a small boy was seen, as well as other places around the area. As the legend goes, one of the nuns had a nephew named Monroe living with her. Sometime in the early 1900s, Monroe was killed by a train and was buried in the cemetery located on the academy grounds. The spirit of the child has since been believed to be Monroe.

A disappearing noose was seen hanging on the fire escape, only to be gone when the two researchers who saw it brought additional witnesses. Steven LaChance, founder of MPR, saw the apparition of a woman with a noose around her neck climb out of a window onto the fire escape, only to disappear. Shadows were seen walking the balcony by several others, as were balls of light. The odor of sulfur was detected again, shortly after Steven made the comment, "Demonic priest"!

Investigators managed to follow the horrid smell as it moved up the steps, as if walking, until it faded away.

By far the most ominous encounter started around 3:00 A.M., known by most investigators as the demonic hour. Often, in demonic cases, activity seems to heighten around 3:00 A.M., which is the opposite of the time Christ is believed by some to have been born.

During that hour, Tim Clifton prepared to leave as he had

another appointment later that morning. As he said his goodbyes, there was the sound of moving furniture upstairs in the attic. As Tim describes, "It's not just a chair being moved, these sounds were loud!" Steven looked at Tim, knowing he couldn't leave now.

The two spiritual warriors went into the attic. Tim said the room was full of shadow people who broke and ran "like a Chinese fire drill."

Tim reported the shadows scrambled about, disappearing into the walls. Up a small stairway was a little door which they were told went to the widow's walk. A widow's walk is an area on older homes, often equipped with a hand railing, usually seen on the East Coast, designed so wives could walk up to the widow's walk, and watch for their husbands' ship to return to harbor.

Steven called for more investigators to come up. From behind the small door they could hear a knocking sound.

Tim, without thinking, opened it for whoever may be up there. Suddenly, a dark black cloud swept out of the open door leaving a feeling of pure evil behind it. Steven attempted to pick up Tim, who was standing in the path of the black mass. It swirled around him, passing into a closet. Greg Myers, investigator and co-administrator of MPR, opened the door as Tim photographed. According to Tim Clifton, the photos showed the doorframe, and blackness just inside the door as Greg stepped inside. Pure black—where Greg seemed to have disappeared inside.

During an EVP session, the question was asked "Are you a priest?" The answer was, "I was a priest." Strangely, the answer was heard only on the recording as with most EVPs, but it was heard just before the question was asked!

Photographs showed white mists that appeared to be a woman in early 1900's clothing looking out of a window and, of course, the blackness of the closet, which disappeared in later photos. Members heard discussions in the hallway between men and women unseen by the living eye plus the sound of movement in empty rooms. Few, if any, of the team members slept that night. So much for the recreational Casper hunt!

For the amateur ghost hunter, Arcadia Valley is a great destination for a weekend hunt. Plenty of history. Sites to see include Elephant Rocks, Johnson's Shut-ins and, of course, the paranormal hunts in all three cities.

It seems every place has its own story to tell. Whether it's in the comfortable Parlor Bed and Breakfast or on the recorder with the ghostly voice of a long-dead priest, all have tales to tell.

It is portentous and a thing of state,
that here at midnight in our little town
A mourning figure walks and will not rest,
Near the old courthouse, pacing up and down.

—Vachel Lindsay
1879-1931
American Poet, known as the 'Prarie Troubador'

ODA MAE BROWN: He's stuck, that's what it is. He's in between worlds. You know it happens sometimes that the spirit gets yanked out so fast that the essence still feels it has work to do here.

—Ghost, 1990

Photo by Dan Terry

The Lemp Mansion Restaurant *stands as a sinister reminder of the wealthy St. Louis beer family that once called the mansion home, that is, until they ended their lives intentionally.*

St. Louis City, Missouri

Chapter 3

St. Louis Royalty

now and forever, the Lemp family is not ready to leave the mansion

If any family in the history of St. Louis could be called royalty, it would be the Lemp family. They had money to burn, a mansion, the newest and fanciest gadgets to make life easy, everything anyone could want. Except happiness.

Adam Lemp was an immigrant with a dream. He had learned the art of making beer while in Germany and, in 1838, came to America, following the promise of a right to pursue happiness. Adam started a small grocery store and made beer in the back room, starting his own saloon.

What Adam learned was unexpected. For those who were used to drinking the dark, heavy, bitter British ales, this new lager beer, lighter and sharper, appealed to the American taste. Adam Lemp was to become a millionaire and form an aristocracy to rival the East Coast "old money" people.

Adam had ice cut from the Mississippi River and placed in a

shed, packed in sawdust, because lagering requires beer to be kept at 35 to 49 degrees while conditioning. Eventually, Adam closed down his grocery store and moved the factory to an area where he had access to the extensive cave system hiding beneath St. Louis.

William Lemp, the eldest son of Adam, came to St. Louis with his parents at age 12. He attended St. Louis University then joined the Union Army at the outbreak of the Civil War. After his discharge, and after the death of his father, William became the head of the Lemp brewing empire.

While his father may have been satisfied with being the top brewer in St. Louis, William had a keen business sense and a drive to succeed. William began expanding the brewery, which eventually needed five city blocks to house the entire operation. By 1878, the William J. Lemp Brewing Company was producing more than 100,000 barrels of beer a year, and had its own trains and refrigerated cars to transport the beer from coast to coast. As with the families of European royalty, Lemp's daughter would marry into the Pabst family, of Pabst Blue Ribbon beer fame.

But William Lemp had an appetite for more than just a place in the beer business. He married Julia Feickert and their marriage produced nine children. William bought the house built by Julia's father, and enlarged it to become what is today known as the Lemp Mansion.

The Lemp Mansion, while large before William bought it, was turned into a 33-room showplace. In 1884, not long after radiant heat was patented, the house boasted radiators in all rooms. A staircase was removed from the two-story home, and was replaced with one of the first elevators in St. Louis, running from the basement to the second floor. Italian marble was used for decorative mantles, as well as African mahogany, and the ceiling was hand painted. Perhaps the most extravagant of all, in an era when most homes did not have indoor plumbing, a shower using jets from above and three sides was purchased from a hotel in Italy and transported to St. Louis for Lemp's personal use.

For Julia, William Lemp built an atrium where she could sit away from the nine children. The round room with many windows boasted exotic plants and rare birds flying free.

Here the royal heads of Europe were entertained, along with

the Who's Who of the new American Republic. In the caves that ran from the mansion to the brewery a block away, heated shallow pools were constructed for the entertainment of the family and their elite guests, and a stage was built for private plays and musicals. This was the heyday of the Lemp family, as close to American royalty as we would see until the Kennedy clan. However, the family was cursed to lose it all within a generation.

While William Lemp Jr. was the oldest son, William Sr. pinned the family's hopes on Frederick. As the younger William played the role of the playboy millionaire's son, Frederick, who was an intense, driven man similar to William Sr., worked and studied. He attended Washington University, earning an engineering degree, and then began studying to take over the family business. Believing in the potential for this favorite son to guide the family business into the 20th century, the elder William was secure.

In 1901, however, Frederick Lemp died suddenly of a heart attack at the age of 28. It was popularly believed that he had worked himself to death, taking into account the amount of time he spent in the brewery and working on the future of Lemp Beer.

The death of his favorite son sent William Sr. into a slow tailspin. He went into a deep depression, now walking to work in the tunnels below instead of on the sunny street above. No longer walking the line or speaking with the employees, he began spending more and more time alone. His only real interest seemed to be the extravagant mausoleum he had built in tribute to his fallen son. While on the planning committee for the famous 1904 World's Fair to be held in St. Louis, his participation in the meetings slowly decreased.

Then, one cold morning in February 1904, William Lemp Sr. went downstairs for breakfast while his wife was out shopping, telling the servants he was feeling unwell.

After breakfast, he went upstairs, locked the bedroom door, and the first of four suicides in the family took place. The elder William shot himself in the head behind the locked door. His sons, William Jr. and Edwin, were summoned from the brewery. They kicked in the door and found their father lying on the floor, gun in hand, but still breathing. The family doctor was summoned but the elder William's wound was too extreme. William J. Lemp Sr. died as his wife returned from shopping. The second domino fell in the short line of the brewery empire.

William Jr. took over the family business. As his father may have feared, William began spending vast amounts of money on servants, country estates, fancy carriages and a large art collection. He married Lillian, a woman from a wealthy family, who also loved to spend money. Known by the press at the time as the "Lavender Lady", it was widely believed that she was not much more than a trophy wife. They had one child, William III.

While William Jr. spent money on trinkets and show, the competition was building newer breweries with state-of-the-art equipment. A messy divorce ensued and the Lavender Lady moved to New York.

In 1905, William Jr.'s beloved mother was diagnosed with cancer, and spent the final days of her life in the mansion living in intense pain. She died in the summer of 1906 in the family home.

As the movement toward Prohibition gained momentum in the Midwest, Lemp Brewery sought to make a non-alcoholic beer called Cerva, but it was a financial failure. In 1911, he converted the family home into offices for the brewery, living instead at one of the farms he purchased. In 1915, he remarried, this time to a formidable-looking widow named Ellie. As the first wife was a model, spoiled and rich, this one resembled Ma Kettle.

When Prohibition was enacted by Congress, William Lemp Jr. had had enough. In 1919, Lemp stopped producing his near beer, and closed the factory without warning. Employees showed up for work to find locked gates. William sold the Falstaff beer name for only $25,000 and the brewery, worth $7 million, was sold to International Shoe Co. for a paltry $600,000. The William J. Lemp Brewery was as dead as its founder.

The curse, however, was not finished. Although the family was still very wealthy, sister Elsa Lemp-Wright shot herself to death in her St. Louis home in 1920. There is some question as to a suicide, as she had recently reconciled with the husband she had earlier divorced after a rocky marriage and had re-married him only two weeks earlier. Her husband, Thomas Wright, claimed he was preparing to bathe when he heard the gunshot. He found Elsa in bed, the gun in her hand. He called the doctor but she died before he arrived. However, William Jr. seemed to have no doubt. When he arrived, he was told about the incident and reportedly said, "That's the Lemp family for you."

Possibly feeling guilty because he had been in charge of the brewery when it failed, William Lemp Jr. began sliding into a depression much as his father had done after Frederick's death. On December 29, 1922, William went to his office, placed a revolver against his chest, and pulled the trigger. He died in his office before the doctor could get there, ending any hope that the Lemp Brewery would make a comeback.

The funeral was held December 31. As with his father and mother, the funeral was held in the family home. The days of the Lemp name being connected with beer were over. Strangely enough, when Prohibition was lifted, Falstaff® beer became the first licensed beer to begin production. The main beer of the Lemp brewery continued, as did the family curse.

William Lemp III lost his father's country home when it was foreclosed on in 1934. He was divorced in 1936 and died in 1943, having never recovered from the failure of his father. The first American Camelot had passed into history.

William Jr.'s brother, Charles, moved back into the mansion around 1930. He committed suicide in the mansion in 1949, being the only one of the family to leave a note. Rather than be interred in the family mausoleum, he was cremated and his brother, Edwin, was the only one who knew where the ashes were buried. Edwin died of natural causes in 1970, and the Lemp family would never be heard from again. At least while living . . .

Today, the mansion still stands, having been turned into a boarding house in the mid-century and the elevator replaced with a staircase. The neighborhood deteriorated as well. The wonderful old homes were taken over by the homeless, the drug addicts, and the castaways of society as a flop house. In the 70's, the old house was purchased and returned to its former glory, given new life as a bed and breakfast and top class restaurant.

As for the Lemp family, they are still represented by the spirits that haunt the mansion. In the November 1980 issue of *Life* magazine, the mansion was listed as one of the top ten haunted destinations in the U.S. Recently, the Travel Channel has listed the mansion as number two. Famous ghost author Troy Taylor, who has written some 50 books on the paranormal, takes overnight tours several times a year in which investigators can hunt the haunters all evening. His books include *Haunted Illinois, Haunted St. Louis,* and *Devil Came to St. Louis,* which is about the possession of a child by satanic forces upon which the blockbuster movie, "The Exorcist," was based.

I spent an evening on one of Taylor's overnights at the Lemp Mansion. The degree to which he has researched the history of the mansion and the Lemp family is incredible. Many of the other ghost tours he provides, including Haunted Alton, Haunted Chicago, and the Bell Witch are historically accurate and equally entertaining.

I had been to the Lemp Mansion with St. Louis Spirit Search in 2000. Betsy Belanger, director and chief guide, is a firecracker of a woman, with a sunny attitude that belies her work in a haunted house.

That time, the attic was an undone mess of plaster and side boards hanging from the wall studs. We were introduced to two spirits of the house, Zeke and the dog. Betsy said that there was a spirit of a boy, who was mentally challenged and large for his age, and who was the son of William Sr. and Julia. The boy grew and played in the attic, being cared for by the servants. Another spirit was that of a large, black dog owned by Charles, who shot the animal prior to killing himself. The main spirit there seems to be William Jr., whom Betsy identifies as "Billy".

On our return to the Mansion with Troy Taylor, he said he did not believe in Zeke or the ghostly dog, as there was no evidence that either existed.

I took one more tour of the mansion with Betsy, this time in early 2008. Betsy was still a fireball of energy, speaking on the history of the mansion as if she were family. Since my first tour, Betsy has become a celebrity in the paranormal world, having been on National Geographic Television, the Fox Family Channel's "Real Scary Stories", MTV's "Fear", and Discovery Channel's "A Haunting".

Betsy has increased the frequency of the tours from once a month to once a week, giving them each Monday evening. The bed and breakfast there allows people to stay in the rooms with no caretaker present, just you and the ghost. On this evening, a young newlywed couple would be staying alone in the building after the tour. Betsy said they would be given a map out and a place to leave the key if their fear drove them out.

While people have left suddenly in the night before, Betsy says the ghosts in the mansion are happy. She is in contact with Billy, or William Jr., and speaks with him during the tour, using dowsing rods. These are two foot-long slim copper rods, bent into an 'L' shape, and when held in the hand, can move apart for "yes", or cross each other for "no" when asking simple questions of the ghost. On this tour, as with the last one, Betsy spoke with Billy prior to starting the tour.

Betsy believes there are seven spirits living within the house. Five are Lemp family members including Julia, the mother of Billy, William Jr. and brother Zeke. In addition, there are at least two other spirits, a 40-ish female nanny known as Sarah, whom she describes as a very pleasant woman, and Elizabeth, a nine-year-old girl who died while the place was a boarding house in the 50's. Research reveals no murders, but Betsy believes Elizabeth died violently, probably in an accident.

Betsy was on a television show with noted psychic Sylvia Brown, who believes there are two more ghosts, whom Betsy calls Martha and Naomi. Others have seen ghosts that cannot be attributed to the other seven, and Betsy believes these may be the ones. There is also Charles's dog, and several cats that used to play in the atrium.

Betsy has related stories of her employees and mansion employees running into people upstairs—people who disappeared when spoken to. There have also been several incidents when people who were eating in the restaurant had directed the waitress to a lone man sitting at another table, saying he was there first. However, the man disappears before his order can be taken. Other waitresses have spoken to the man at the table, who promptly vanishes. According to accounts, some employees have left at that moment, never to return.

When the mansion was a boarding house, Betsy related, two foreign men living there began throwing things out the windows, screaming in their own language until the police arrived, placing both of them into a mental health facility. A young woman living there with her husband later met with one of the men, who claimed they were kept in the institution for a week because they swore the mansion had a demon. Neither would return.

In October 2001, the Dave Glover show, a local radio show hosted by St. Louis radio personality Dave Glover, did their annual all-night ghost show in the Lemp Mansion. That time, after Glover made a remark about the boy, there was an audible EVP heard across radios all over mid Missouri and Illinois, with the ghostly voice demanding "I'm Zeke!"

While the controversy over the existence of Zeke rages on, one thing that cannot be disputed is that there are ghosts in the mansion. Each trip, I have photographed extremely bright orbs climbing the stairway in almost the same place each time. This time, while Betsy had the tour upstairs in the newly refinished attic, attempting to coax Zeke from his chosen place in one of the rooms, I observed two shadow people quickly move across the hall. One went back and peeked around the corner.

A short time later, several people, including Sherri, saw another shadow person peek around the corner from the room we were in. While Betsy was speaking at the beginning of the tour, we got an EMF reading on the table, reading very high just before she began speaking to Billy. The reading returned to zero, and we could not find it again. Maybe Billy was looking at my notes, checking for accuracy!

Ghost hunters can sign up for the historical tour with Troy Taylor, or the more fun tour with Betsy. Either is well worth the time, even for non-believers interested only in local history or the incredible architecture of the building.

For the especially brave, stay a night alone in the mansion. If you make it to breakfast, I'm sure it will be wonderful.

A ghost is someone who hasn't made it—in other words, who died, and they don't know they're dead. So they keep walking around and thinking that you're inhabiting their—let's say, their domain. So they're aggravated with you.

—Sylvia Browne

Photo by Dan Terry

Guests at the historic Arlington Hotel in DeSoto, Missouri, *have ranged from Jefferson Davis to Billy Joel. The building has served a multitude of purposes, ranging from a railroad hotel, halfway house, brothel, bar and restaurant. Although this beautiful structure has found new life after renovation, not all of the guests sign the register.*

Chapter 4

A Divine Haunting

do angels patrol the halls of this former brothel?

There have been a lot of visitors to the Arlington Hotel over its long history. Wrestler Andre the Giant, Singer Billy Joel, Actor James Arness of 'Gunsmoke' fame, Eleanor Roosevelt, even the President of the Confederacy Jefferson Davis, have all stayed at the Arlington in DeSoto, Missouri. Its checkered history includes a railroad hotel, halfway house for convicts, brothel, bar and restaurant. Could it now be an earthly station for angels?

DeSoto began as a wilderness, obtained by the upstart Americans through the Louisiana Purchase. In 1803, the first known settler, Isaac Von Metre, built his log cabin on the banks of Joachim Creek. That property changed hands several times in what is now the City of Desoto, as more people settled in the area.

In 1818, Jefferson County was formed and named in honor of the third President of the United States. In 1859, the Iron Mountain Railroad built a depot in DeSoto, which brought about population growth. Later, they built a railroad car repair shop that became, and remains, one of the largest employers in the area.

DeSoto was incorporated in 1869, named for Hernando de Soto, the explorer who had earlier claimed this area for Spain. The town would also become known as Fountain City for the many artesian wells in the area. The water was shipped, bottled, and even used to supply the 1904 World's Fair in St. Louis.

A native of DeSoto, Thomas Fletcher, became a colonel in the Union Army during the Civil War. He commanded African American troops in the battle for Pilot Knob, was brevetted brigadier general and then, in 1864, was elected Governor of Missouri.

Because the railroad had been completed through DeSoto, troops and supplies were being shipped through the town to Pilot Knob. At one point, the Confederate battle flag, the Stars and Bars, was raised on a makeshift pole over DeSoto by Southern sympathizers. However, upon the arrival of a trainload of Union soldiers, the flag and pole were hastily removed. According to local legend, the soldiers found the Rebel symbol under the butt of a woman who was sitting on a bench in an attemp to hide the flag.

The town saw growth. In addition to the railroad car shop, a brick factory provided additional employment and brought more people to the thriving village. DeSoto was featured in *Look* as the All-American City in 1954 and 1959, and had the honor of being declared the population center of the United States in 1980.

The Arlington, originally known as Desoto House, was built along the railroad tracks in the 1860's. It offered 50 tiny sleeping rooms, each containing a bed and small table, designed for railroad workers who needed to catch a quick nap between trains. As rail travel was replaced by automobiles and planes, the hotel slowly fell into disuse and disrepair.

For a time, it served as a halfway house, offering shelter to former convicts. The building was also used as a boarding house and, as was the case with many old railroad hotels, it became a brothel. During the era when it was occupied by convicts and drug addicts, the third floor caught fire and was gutted. Soon, the structure was uninhabitable and left to the elements.

Eventually, Dennis and Judy Welsh purchased the building, rescuing it from a scheduled demolition. They began the expensive process of restoration, using old photographs as a guide. Dennis rebuilt the upstairs, making the walls thicker and creating 17 spacious rooms where 50 tiny rooms had once been.

Ron and Diana Johnson now own the Arlington. Linda Mason, Diana's sister, tells a story about the time when Diana, as a child, had found an old perfume bottle that had become buried in the soil and weathered for many years. Diana restored the bottle slowly, carefully and, in doing so, developed a love for antiques. In 2002, Diana discovered the Arlington, and immediately fell in love with the old building. Today, Diana and Ron run the Arlington with people staying there by the night or by the week, and they operate the restaurant as well.

In April 2008, I stepped into the restaurant and spoke with an attractive black-haired waitress. I asked to speak with the owner and explained my mission. At the mention of ghosts, the waitress rolled her eyes.

You don't believe in ghosts?" I asked. She smiled. "I think it's haunted. The cook thinks it's haunted. But the owner, well, she owns the place."

I was directed to Diana, who was in the restaurant working on a reservation. When I told her what I was there for, Diana smiled the same kind of smile.

"Oh, I don't think there are ghosts here," Diana said. "but there are angels!"

I've had people agree their place is haunted, deny their place is haunted, and ask me not to talk about their place being haunted. This answer was surprising.

"The people who owned this before us, Dennis and Judy Welsh, had a blessing done to run the ghosts out." Diana explained. "Dennis used to do his own cleansing each week. They asked that angels be sent to protect the building and they do.

"Then when we took over," she went on, "We had a minister come in. He prayed for an army of angels to guard the building."

Since then, Diana, along with others, has reported feeling the presence of angels in the building. Some have even seen them.

Diana related several stories of people seeing the angels, even before she bought the Arlington. One little girl, the daughter of a local businessman, swore she saw an angel sitting in the Lavender Room, which Diana believes is a favorite place of her angelic guardians.

"One night, a Catholic nurse staying here was unable to sleep and got up at 3:00 A.M. to pray. She claimed she had been given a revelation and would change her life completely," Diana related. "That same night, a couple was staying here from the area. The wife was originally from India. She came down after the nurse left and said that she was sure the Holy Spirit had been on that floor that night. She said she suddenly felt a most peaceful calm around 3:00 A.M. Neither of the women knew or had spoken with the other."

"One Christmas, the young granddaughter of the Welsh family, the previous owners, was reaching skyward as if wanting to to be picked up. No one was there. She said it was an angel! Then, someone took a photo and there was a bright orb right where she was reaching!"

Are the angels protecting the Arlington? "Once a coven of witches showed up. They had done a séance in the area, and stopped for a meal.

"As they approached, the leader stopped at the door. The waitress noticed them standing by the door, and went over to them. The leader of the coven asked if they could eat on the porch. Of course, we didn't care. But I went out to ask why. The head witch, or whatever, said 'Do you know there are angels walking around here?"

In another instance, a male witch had entered the restaurant and began walking down the halls. Diana said, "He was reaching up, grabbing at the air." She demonstrated by extending her arms upward and pinching lightly with her thumb and index fingers. "I asked what he was doing, and he said 'Did you know there are angels here?' He told me he was touching their energy."

When I spoke with the waitress, she told a story with a different flavor. "One day, I placed a plate of cucumber slices on this table," She indicated a table in the restaurant near the salad bar. "I went back into the kitchen and heard a loud crash. When I ran back into the empty room, the whole plate had flown off the table and hit the wall there." She pointed at the outside wall which was about 12 feet from the table.

Angels or ghosts—something stalks the halls of the old Arlington Hotel in downtown DeSoto. Diana said that in a few days, a paranormal group had rented the building for a night of investigation. Others have told her they felt a divine presence in the building.

You'll have to go to the Arlington yourself to know for sure. But remember, it seems the angels don't care for cucumbers.

. . . Oh God! Do you think I want to be a ghost?

—John V.A. Weaver
Poet, 1893-1938

Photos by Dan Terry

Above: ***The Prosperity School Bed and Breakfast*** *on the outskirts of Joplin*

Left: Second Floor of the Prosperity School Bed & Breakfast. Note orbs playing near Miss Pink's room (in hallway).

Jasper County, Missouri

Chapter 5

Where Recess Never Ends

the Prosperity School Bed and Breakfast, where the school fun lasts forever

Childhood. Springtime of our lives. When we had no responsibility, and the world belonged to us. Will you ever have friends as close as those in your childhood? Who wouldn't want to go back to elementary school, when running and playing was the major concern, giggling at our best friend's joke while trying to hide the conversation from the teacher, the simplicity of play . . .

Joplin, Missouri, lies in the southwest corner of the state. Jasper County was named for a Revolutionary War hero, Sgt. William Jasper, who recovered the American flag after the pole was shot down, and waved it as the troops rallied to defeat the British.

The county was established in 1841 and the first county seat was around the kitchen table of the split log home of George Hornbeck, situated on the bluffs above the Spring River. The first county court was also held in this residence.

In 1907, the residents of the small mining town of Prosperity, on the outskirts of Joplin, decided their children needed a school. In Prosperity Township, a brick two-story building was put up and called the Prosperity School. Classes were held here from 1907 until 1962, when the school system was consolidated into the Webb City School District.

In its day, the school held some 1200 students. When business with the local mines began to decline, so did the population. Slowly, the many churches, saloons, and businesses moved to Joplin and other more populated places. When the school finally closed its doors, there were only 32 students.

The building sat idle for more than 30 years. In the late 1990s, it was restored as a bed and breakfast, more as a labor of love than with hopes of a large financial gain. Although the slate chalk boards have been removed, the wooden chalk trays still circle many of the rooms. The hardwood floors still proudly boast of its history, with the marks of desks and tables and the dents of daily use still visible. In the silence of the night, one can still almost hear the laughter and play of the hundreds of children who played and learned in those great halls.

Almost? For Richard and Janet Roberts, owners and innkeepers of the Prosperity School Bed and Breakfast, the memories of the past don't just linger there, but run, play, talk, and make themselves known in a variety of ways.

Nearly six years ago, Richard and Janet purchased the restored building to use as a bed and breakfast. The previous owners did not tell them of the spirits within its halls, possibly fearing they would change their minds. Obviously, they did not know the Roberts family that well.

Richard and Janet have gone miles out of their way searching for haunted places. The Crescent Hotel and Spa in Eureka Springs, Arkansas, the Myrtles Plantation in Louisiana, and the Lodge in Cloudcroft, New Mexico have been just a few of the haunted inns they stayed in prior to buying this one. It was more than a pleasant surprise when they learned that their new home was haunted as well.

"We're starting to amass repetitive stories here." Janet told me as she handed me an eleven-page summary of the haunting reports at the school. "Right after we opened, guests started telling us their experiences, and I decided to start writing them down as a journal of the building."

In the past couple of years, this building has housed such notable names in the paranormal field as John Zaffis, noted demonologist, Chris Moon, editor and chief of *Haunted Times Magazine;* and TAPS (The Atlantic Paranormal Society) founders Jason Hawes and Grant Wilson of TV's "Ghost Hunters" fame. Chris Moon, using his "Telephone to the Dead", uncovered several spirits in the building including a teacher and a small girl.

Richard and Janet bought the building in November, 2002, and

Richard had an encounter with a shadow person shortly after that, but shrugged it off at the time to overwork. The first encounter written about in the haunting history Janet provided me occurred in January 2003, when a guest asked if they had been knocking on their door at night. Each time the lady checked, the hallway outside was empty. At first the guest thought her grown daughter may have been doing this, but dismissed the idea as being too childish.

The haunting stories continued up through early June 2008. One story she had not yet added involved Janet getting an intense feeling of fear when she went to shut off some lights. Janet attributes this to the possible presence of the former custodian, Walden Bullis.

Janet knew there was at least one adult spirit as well as children in her home. Once, while in the shower, she heard a male voice as if he was clearing his throat. Richard was in another room at the time. Another time, while cleaning the room after the guest had left, Janet asked Richard, who was behind her, if he had read the nice comment the previous guest had written in their book. Richard answered, "no". Then, Janet heard a male voice ask, "Why?" Thinking that this was a strange answer from her husband, she looked back at him. "What do you mean 'why'?" she asked. He denied saying "why?", or even hearing it.

Confirmation occurred when some former students told her about Walden. A family member of the late custodian reported that each night, he would come in through the back door, check the entire building, and exit through the front door. This explains the late night heavy footsteps upstairs, shadows seen passing the kitchen door, and the occasional lights being found on during the night.

Creaks in the floor as if someone is walking upstairs even when the house is all but empty, doors opening and closing by themselves, hearing children speaking in hushed, classroom gossip tones, even piano music playing children's tunes reported by caretakers and guests alike. One retired school teacher left this note in the book: ". . . As a retired teacher, I love the atmosphere. I heard kids reciting their multiplication facts last night."

Richard and Janet have also reported hearing the sound of metal pipes being worked on as if someone was working on the plumbing. "Tink . . . Tink . . . Tink Tink . . . " all within the floors. However, there was no indoor plumbing when it was a school, and PVC pipes were used when it was rebuilt.

In July 2004, Janet went to the kitchen to place the juice pitcher in the refrigerator to chill for breakfast. However, even though the house was empty except for her and she had just made the juice, the pitcher was gone. To this day, it has not been found.

The Roberts' dog has had plenty of experiences of her own. She's been found outside the bedroom door of the Pink Room, one of the most active rooms, barking into the empty chamber, his back hair standing up. She's also been found in a chair barking at the open door of another room, keeping her distance but alerting her owners to the intruder unseen by human eyes.

Richard and Janet recently heard loud footsteps coming down the hallway as they worked in the kitchen. Believing the guests had arrived early, they went out to greet them. No one was in the hallway. On June 13, Richard was up at 2:30 A.M. sitting in the hallway, when he heard movement upstairs as if someone was up there. The sounds continued steadily for 30 minutes. Janet has also witnessed moving shadows, one very short, and has heard the creaking noises in the floor overhead. She no longer bothers to investigate.

Eager to share the spirits, the Prosperity School Bed and Breakfast has hosted a number of paranormal research groups. The Ghost Hunters from Missouri Southern State University uses their home for training new members. Northwest Arkansas Ghost Connection, Southeast Kansas Paranormal Investigators, Tri-County Paranormal Research, CASPR, and others have investigated the building and none have gone home disappointed. One team had recordings of two sets of footsteps on the floor above them, one heavy-booted, the other described as the clicky sound from ladies' high heels.

Others have gotten photographs of mirrors showing strange looking anomalies that cannot be explained. One team from the college reported two female members waking up from the exact same dream, in which each was playing hide-and-seek with a small child in the bedroom. When one of the women looked up, she heard a giggle and saw the bathroom door close by itself! Guests have reported getting what they called 'extreme goose bumps' on one side of their body. Teams have gotten many orbs and light or energy streaks across the photograph. One investigator set up motion sensors within Miss Pink's room, aimed at the door. From the bathroom, she heard the alarm go off, and immediately investigated. While standing there, the alarm went off a second time. Checking the area with the EMF detector, the investigator said the needle began swinging wildly from side to side, something she had never seen before. The investigator's husband had also been awakened from a deep sleep earlier by a strange tapping noise coming from the window. The pair then spent the rest of the night up and investigating the second floor, encountering a short, dark shadow crossing the floor in front of them.

A newlywed couple experienced a visitation while using the large whirlpool tub. The bride had sensed that someone had entered the guest room, even though the door was locked. As she turned toward the door, a small black shadow crossed the room, disappearing into the wall. Another couple reported hearing what they described as a "small body" falling to the floor with a loud clump, followed by the excited voices of small children. One mother, who was staying there with her husband, told Janet she had felt her foot touched, then a small hand taking her own in the gentle grip of a loving child.

Light bulbs exploding, lights turning on and off, sometimes seemingly burning out only to come back on a day later. These are some of the experiences from the owners, guests and paranormal investigators that visit the B and B. In April 2007, the Tri-County Paranormal investigators checked the Prosperity School and took an incredible photo of what appears to be a ghostly nurse.

The Tri-County Paranormal team started with Tom Faris and his son, Ernie, Tom's daughter Melissa Fisher, and friend Tiffany Campbell. Today, the team, which began in February 2007, boasts six members and have investigated all over the Midwest.

I spoke with Melissa Fisher about their investigations at the Prosperity School Bed and Breakfast. Melissa Fisher is an officer with the Anderson, Missouri Police Department and also works as a nurse and deputy with the Jasper County Sheriff's Department.

"We've had lots of personal experiences." Melissa said. She described setting up a video camera, hooked to a laptop, and the screen would black out on command of Tiffany, as if a spirit or shadow person stepped in front of it when she asked. The camera was later taken to an expert, who proclaimed it was working perfectly.

On the last investigation, Melissa's brother, Ernie, asked a question upstairs at the school and while going over the evidence heard an EVP consisting of a female voice telling him, "I love you."

But in April 2007, Melissa took a photo that the owners of the

Photo by Melissa Fisher, co-founder of Tri-County Paranormal

There should only be a wall showing in this photograph, taken at the Prosperity School Bed and Breakfast yet, in the glass door, one can discern a spirit wearing a white top with a black strap over the shoulder.

Prosperity School are very happy with. It appears to show a dark-haired young woman standing in the door, as if a reflection. She appears to be wearing a white coat and seems to have a strap coming down her right shoulder, as if carrying a stethoscope or possibly a purse with a long strap. No one was standing there at the time.

Chris Moon, founder and president of *Haunted Times Magazine,* uses a device known as the 'Telephone to the Dead', or more commonly as 'Frank's Box'. In short, a man named Frank contacted Moon, saying that with spirit help he had completed a device for speaking directly to the dead that Thomas Edison had been working on at the time of his demise. Once finished, the spirits had instructed him to give the box to Moon, which he did without any form of payment.

The voices coming from the box have been uncannily correct with predictions and identifying themselves as deceased family members. Today, Chris Moon travels with the box giving people readings, contacts, and closure with contact from the other side.

While at the bed and breakfast, Moon and some college students used the box to make contact with the spirits there. What came across the waves was that there were six ghosts in the building and some come and go. One is Sadie, a six-year-old girl who reportedly died after a fall down some stairs in 1906. Also making contact were children Theresa, Benjamin, and Billy, and a woman who identified herself as a schoolteacher named Ann. Ann made the comment that her man had given her a black eye.

After considering that for a short time, Janet recalled seeing something on one of the photographs she had managed to find of a school class there. Hanging in the hallway today is a photograph of the 1935 Prosperity class, along with their young, attractive school teacher who appears to have a very dark circle around her right eye. There are no names on the photo, and records have been impossible to locate since the school closed some 40 years ago. Could the young lady in the photo have been Ann, still hurting from the beating she had received from the man she loved?

When I arrived at the Prosperity School B & B one hot day in late June, I was met by Richard and Janet, who had written accounts of the ghostly experiences and the key to Miss Pink's room, the most haunted room. After speaking with the Roberts, I was introduced to Nick Corey, founder of the paranormal group, Jasper Haunts.

Nick Corey is author of two books on the paranormal, entitled *Electronic Voice Phenomena* and his soon-to-be-released, *The Many Messages,* which deals with contact with the other side through EVP's. He has psychic abilities stretching back through his family line to a famous ancestor.

Giles Corey and this third wife, Martha, were living near Salem, Massachusetts at the time of the witch trials. Martha refused to give any credence to such nonsense, much to the dismay of the judges and township.

Martha and Giles were eventually accused of witchcraft. Martha denied this, but was found guilty and hanged in September 1692. During the hysteria of the time, Giles refused to plead either guilty or not guilty. Some believe that this was due to a loophole in the law that stated if a man was found guilty or pled guilty, his land and property would be seized.

The downside was that, at the time, a suspect had to plead one way or the other, or receive "piene forte et dure", or suffer the torture of pressing. On Monday, September 19, 1692, Giles Corey was given one last chance to plead guilty. Remaining mute, he was placed on the ground, a heavy board placed on his body, and large stones were heaped on the board, slowly pressing him to death. His last words were only a request to add more weight quickly. Giles Corey died there, but his lands and property went to his family rather than to the local sheriff.

Whether Giles or Martha actually practiced witchcraft is unknown.

However, their descendant firmly believes he has inherited some magical skills from the family. Nick Corey is a paranormal investigator and had obtained some of the best evidence I have ever seen, mostly involving the Prosperity School building.

Nick's EVP's include one young spirit that seems to have followed him from the school to his own home. Nick complained that his bowls seem to disappear from his cabinet, similar to the pitcher of juice Janet mentioned. Nick then played a recording:

NICK: *"Which spirit is taking our bowls?"*
CHILD'S VOICE: *"I want some cereal."*

Nick reported that, after that session, he has kept a box of Cocoa Puffs on his table, and the bowls have remained on the shelf.

Nick also claims a long distance (from the other side) relationship with a spirit named Eva. For eight months, Eva gave him information and suggestions from the other side. He played an EVP with what he believed to be Eva's voice making one request: "Record for me."

Another voice captured at the B & B was a woman saying "We aren't living. Am I dead?" "Can see the light. We can see clearly." And on June 21, 2008, "We're not home."

During one EVP session, Janet Roberts asked, "Are there any Civil War soldiers? Any Civil War officers? Civilians?"

A voice came across, right over the microphone, which said "Dr. Plois." Research showed a Dr. Ploy was attached to a Virginia unit during the Civil War.

Nick has received the names of Debbie Raulus and others. After hearing several of the EVP's, it was time to move to the video captures.

One taken in the parlor shows the most unusual orb I've ever seen. A flat-topped orb slowly rose in front of the camera, which was sitting on a table. It moved up to the full screen then very slowly moved to the right, stopping at the side of the lens, then moving up at an angle and slowly crossing the view, then disappearing into the wall, again slowly. It seemed to take two minutes for the orb to go from under the camera to disappearing.

Another showed an energy streak coming from a bedroom, snaking out into the hallway and pulling back into the room, but the best was yet to come.

With the camera pointed from inside Miss Pink's room toward the door and hallway, the video shows the shadows of the investigators as they set up the equipment. Suddenly, a gray shadow crosses the doorway, with what appears to be arms swinging and legs walking. The mist, approximately four feet high, crosses the doorway quickly. After viewing the video several times, Nick Corey slowed the video down, stopping it at one point where what seems to be the head of the spirit turns toward the camera. There was the face of a child with dark hair looking into the room as it passed! As with me, Nick had showed the videos in this order to John Zaffis, who admonished him to forget the orbs and energy streaks. This was all he needed.

The short investigation I managed to do yielded nothing so dramatic. Photos showed only a few unremarkable orbs. I set a video camera in the same location, and managed to record what sounded like children mumbling. At one point, you can hear a boy speaking louder, still in a mumble, and what sounds like a little girl giggling.

At breakfast the next morning, other guests heard what I was doing and mentioned their own experiences. They did not know the place was haunted until they overheard our conversation then they came forward with their own stories. The afternoon before they heard what they thought sounded like a chain being dragged across the outer wall of the room. The third time, the husband said he believed it was a lawn sprinkler hitting the side of the wall. The wife asked that he look outside, and that revealed that there were no sprinklers on as this was the wettest summer in recent memory. No limbs were near the building and no work was being done that Sunday afternoon.

No explanation for the sounds.

For the ghost hunter, a stay at the Prosperity School Bed and Breakfast is a must. The obvious happiness of the children in their perpetual recess playing in the halls, along with the teacher and custodian maintaining their duties in keeping the children happy, will soak into your own lives. Take home that sense of childlike wonderment, happiness, and reminders of the necessity of play.

Consider it a lesson.

Photos by Dan Terry

The Diamonds, long a traveler's icon on Route 66, *stands alone and abandoned, or does it? Some of the travelers on that long-gone, dusty trail remain behind at the old Tri-County Truck Stop, waiting for someone to tell their story.*

Franklin County, Missouri

Chapter 6

Devil's Diner

take a rest stop on the highway to hell

Hey Satan, paid my dues
Playing in a rocking band:
Hey Momma, look at me
I'm on my way to the promised land.

- AC/DC "Highway to Hell"

Two far-sighted businessmen shared a dream to connect Chicago, Illinois, and Los Angeles, California, with a highway unlike any other. They believed that by connecting those two cities, small communities along the way would benefit financially and they would reap a substantial profit. The nation would reap inconceivable financial advantage from such a link. Those men were Cyrus Avery of Tulsa, Oklahoma, and John Woodruff of Springfield, Missouri.

Plans for the highway began in 1916, but early efforts met with little support. A young Army captain named Dwight D. Eisenhower, who had been stuck in the mud with his entire command, envisioned the good such a highway could serve for the movement of troops in the event of a national emergency or, God forbid, a second world war. In 1925, Congress gave the green light for the building of such a highway, and the following year, "Route 66" was on its way to becoming a reality.

Unlike the earlier Lincoln and Dixie highways, both of which had basically followed a straight line from Point A to Point B, Route 66 was to cut diagonally across the country, meandering through small communities in the western half of the nation. This would allow small farms to get their crops to market and, of course, bring city money back to the farms. Linking these rural communities gave Route 66 the nickname 'Main Street of America'.

In 1939, Steinbeck wrote "The Grapes of Wrath", chronicling the movement of migrant farmers. Steinbeck referred to Route 66 as the "Mother Road". During the Dust Bowl days, when a series of dust storms assaulted farms in the Bible belt, driving thousands off of their farms from Texas through Kansas and Oklahoma up through the Dakotas and even into Canada, some 200,000 homeless refugees moved down Route 66 heading to California.

During World War II, troops and equipment moved across the United States quickly and easily, unlike the days when Capt. Eisenhower's troops had been mired down in the mud. The highway also afforded the U.S. Government the opportunity to utilize the great Western area where the weather was warmer and drier, for military training and testing. Men from the East would remember the vast, open fields and warm weather of the American West long after the war. Families that had raised their children in the harsh winters of Chicago and the East Coast would use Route 66 to move to warmer climates in New Mexico, Arizona, and eventually California.

One of these was former Marine Captain Bobby Fuller who, shortly after arriving in Los Angeles following a trip down the Mother Road, penned the famous words, "Get your kicks, on Route 66". That song, recorded by Nat King Cole in 1946, was heard in the living rooms of people nationwide, bringing dreams of open road, freedom and adventure.

Some 2400 miles of adventure awaited the traveler going down America's Main Street. Realizing that travelers, no matter how poor, needed food, gasoline and lodging, businessmen began opening garages, gas stations, cheap motels and campgrounds, and finally the small tourist traps. One of these was called the Diamonds.

The Diamonds began as an all night fruit and vegetable stand in Villa Ridge, some 50 miles from St. Louis. It soon evolved into a restaurant, the original building constructed in 1927. That building burned to the ground in 1948. The fire was so big, it shut down Route 66.

Rebuilt, it became "The place to stop" on Route 66, attracting the biggest names, including Al Capone, Marilyn Monroe, and Elvis Presley. One postcard proclaimed it the "Place to Eat and Meet".

But time caught up with the Diamonds, and with Route 66. The asphalt ribbon, necessary for pre-war transportation and the moving of refugees from the dust bowl, was not adequate for the large truck traffic and explosion of private motor vehicle ownership. In 1956, the Federal Aid Highway Act allowed for a four-lane highway to replace Route 66. By the mid seventies, most of the original Mother Road had been bypassed, causing the closing of entire towns. The final nail was hammered into the Route 66 coffin in October 1984, when the last stretch of the historic road was replaced by Interstate-40 in Williams, Arizona.

When Interstate 44 replaced the Mother Road, the owners of the Diamonds bought a patch of land a mile away, on a exit of the new highway. Taking the name and sign with them, the Diamonds officially moved. Today, the second location is also closed, in deference to more modern truck stops and generic fast food stands.

The original Diamonds became the Tri-County Truck Stop, serving truckers for a few more decades. Soon larger chain truck stops began to spring up near the highway, with easier access. By the mid 80's, the all-night restaurant was dependent on the hungry after-bar traffic to stay open.

During the 60's and early 70's, the upstairs section was turned into small rooms and showers for truckers.

According to local legend, the second floor became a haven for hitchhikers, drugs and prostitution. With such a transient group of people, names and faces are not remembered, and actual incidents are recalled through rumor and legend.

Rumors of the truck stop being haunted started at least in the mid 70's. Former MPR Investigator Tim Clifton has made researching the history of the Diamonds his passion.

One former waitress interviewed worked there from 1976 to 1979. During that time, she would refuse to go into the basement. Each time, she felt something was watching her. Sometime, she heard something growl at her in the empty basement. Upstairs, something held her in the restroom, preventing her from pushing the door open. Then, some invisible hand grabbed her braided hair and pulled. When another waitress tried to open the door, she had no trouble doing so and found the other waitress in a panic, with her braid pulled loose from the top of her head.

One of the legends that is difficult to prove is the one surrounding William Bates. Several former employees remember him. Bates was a discharged soldier. Some believed he had been in Vietnam. Others say he was discharged from the service for mental issues. Descriptions of the man are fairly uniform, if equally vague. Tall. Thin. A strange look in his eyes. Hair color and eye color had been forgotten by those questioned.

Management had allowed him to sleep in the basement, doing odd jobs around the truck stop in lieu of pay. Exactly who Bates was, where he came from, or where he went, remains a mystery. How he managed to get the job is also unknown. But people remember one of his traits.

People remember Bates marking off his area of the basement. Anyone who crossed his line would be subjected to having stuff thrown at them. His temper was remembered even when his hair color was not. His fellow employees worked in constant fear of him.

The last memories of Bates are also just memories, legends with no evidence. Bates got into an altercation with a customer. The manager informed Bates that he would have to leave and find another place to live. Bates then threw something, perhaps a knife, at the manager.

The object missed but struck a customer, handle first, in the chest. Again, local legend says the customer was the patriarch of a St. Louis crime family, accompanied by his bodyguards. Others say it was just a man with a lot of friends. Either way, Bates was last seen running out the door with several men in hot pursuit. Whether Bates outran his pursuers or was beaten or killed, remains a mystery.

All of the employees knew of George, the ghost known for moving items in the restaurant. One former waitress mentioned that after a customer had been very loud and rude with her, an entire bowl of soup up-ended itself into the gentleman's lap. George touches the employees and whispers their names. But an incident occurring in the summer of 2006 caused the management to ask for help.

One night, an employee was sent to the basement to get something that was stored there. When the door was opened, a black shadow flew up the stairs, scaring the worker as it disappeared in the kitchen. That's when Missouri Paranormal Research was called in. Because of the size of the building, MPR called my group, Spookstalker, to assist in the investigation.

Karen Brown, who used to own the Diamonds and later worked there for her daughter, had been touched many times by George. She described the touches as gentle and comforting. Karen, along with her daughter, Laurel Brown, gave a tour of the restaurant and building, telling their stories along the way.

Recently, one customer asked Karen if the place was haunted. When she asked why he would ask such a thing, he mentioned that the salt, pepper and ketchup had slid across the table at him. Laurel spoke of the spirit gently speaking her name, and caressing her neck and hair.

But an incident in June 2006 convinced them that the malevolent spirit that had kept to the basement was out. On that evening, a small boy who was walking down the hall to the restroom looked up the stairway as he passed and saw a man holding a woman with a knife to her throat. The child watched as the man, oblivious to his presence, pulled the knife across the throat of the woman, causing blood to gush in a geyser of red. The child screamed and ran back into the crowed restaurant. Several men ran back to the area, only to find a few droplets of red splashed across the wall opposite the stairway. Karen said there were only a few specks, but she knew it was not ketchup, cherry or anything a restaurant owner would be familiar with. And, it was difficult to clean off. Even weeks afterward, some flecks were still there.

A waitress named Jackie told us of an eerie encounter that had occurred the day before our investigation. The mixer had turned itself on, the door to the oven had crashed open with no one around, and she had heard the dish cart being moved around the room even though no one else was there.

While waiting for the restaurant to close prior to the investigation, a group from MPR witnessed a small metal milk pitcher on a shelf over the back counter slowly move itself to the edge and fall onto the floor. George had introduced himself. MPR Co-Administrator Greg Meyers, along with Karen Brown, went into the empty, dark kitchen to attempt an EVP session. When the pots and pans began loudly clanging together, Karen ran out of the kitchen, proclaiming she had heard enough.

That night, I only got a few orbs in the basement, along with one EVP. Groups had been coming through as I attempted a session. When Greg Meyers ordered a lockdown, I mentioned to any spirit that we were alone now, no one to bother us.

Checking the tape later, we distinctly heard the word, "Good", right after I made that statement.

A week later, MPR returned and set up video cameras in the basement as well as upstairs, where psychics believe the spirits of a young, female murder victim, her unborn child, and the murderer still resided. While checking the bathroom, the scene of many ghostly visions, an investigator saw a flash sink into the floor. Checking the cameras in the basement, a blue human-shaped form was seen walking past the camera. This video, greatly debated, made news across the paranormal world. So far, though it has many critics, it has not been proven false.

A few weeks later, members of MPR took a local newspaper reporter through during daylight hours for a story. While down in the basement, a rusty, old knife that had been lying on the floor for years was thrown end-over-end, striking the ductwork near the startled investigators. Was Mr. Bates letting them know they had crossed the barrier to his territory?

The final investigation occurred after the restaurant had closed. Once again, Spookstalker had been called in to assist. My team again settled in the basement. This time, Sherri and I were accompanied by Frank Garren, one of the founding members of Spookstalker and a recent veteran of the battles for Fallujah, Iraq. Upon manning a video camera on nightshot, he found an orb crossing the room at a high rate of speed, then making a right angle turn at 45 degrees, disappearing into the wall. In the next room, I heard Greg Meyers ask the ghost to make a noise for him. In the room we were in, separated from Greg's group by a wall with an open door, a rock struck the back wall and fell to the floor.

I took the video into the next room to inform Greg about the experience. After seeing and hearing the story, Greg proclaimed in a loud voice, "The restaurant is closed. If you don't make a noise for us, we are going to leave, and you'll be alone forever!"

At that moment, every pipe in the basement, whether sewer, water or furnace, seemed to shake with one violent movement. The sound was incredibly loud, made worse with the concrete walls surrounding us. It was as if a bomb had gone off outside the building. Frank, ever the skeptic, proclaimed it had been produced by 'water hammer' and loose pipes.
To prove this, he grabbed a pipe and, using his six-foot plus, 220-pound muscular frame, he attempted to move the pipes but was unable to make it budge.

Sherri and I decided to try our luck upstairs. As we climbed the steps, we passed an ashen-faced Tim Clifton, holding onto the railing.

"Dan", Tim warned, "Be careful up there. The murderer's spirit is up there, and he is mad. I've been slapped, and shoved so hard that if I hadn't been against the wall, I would have been knocked over."

I set up recorders, and began taking photographs. I was surprised at the lack of orbs in the photos. A short time later, Tim came back for round two with five others investigators. Tim immediately began taunting the spirits. I continued to photograph at random. Tim, a Baptist minister, began demanding the spirit show himself. He asked the other spirits—the woman and child—to come to him. Tim called the male spirit a coward, saying that he would only strike a man from the back while intimidating a woman and child.

I continued to photograph. I was amazed that, during this speech to the female and child spirit about the cowardly bully ghost, there were three bright orbs over Tim's head where no orbs had appeared before.

I began watching a human-shaped shadow on the wall to my right. It seemed to be pacing. I watched in silence as Tim continued his ranting against the male ghost. Suddenly, Tim stopped for a few moments then asked, "Does anyone see that shadow?"

The male shadow stopped pacing. There were no windows opposite the wall, only those behind me. Any light would have to have made a right angle turn to flash a shadow on that wall.

But, playing the skeptic, I checked it out anyway. I was unable to interfere with the shadow. I did notice the light from another truck stop visible from the last window. Tim made the comment that he could see my shadow and the other one. What could be making it? After all, we were on the second floor!

"Well, let's just block it and see what happens." I stepped in front of the window. "Now what are you going to do?"

There was a collective gasp from all the other people in the room. Then, in a quiet voice Tim said, "Dan, it's above you."

I had challenged the shadow and it responded by rising above my shadow but remaining on the wall. I returned to my chair and the shadow returned to its location. Tim demanded it come into the room and I saw the shadow get smaller, then larger, as if it went through the window. Others present believe they saw what appeared to be arms and legs come though the window. Either way, it again responded.

It took its place on the wall again, but began to dissipate. When we could no longer see it, we went back downstairs. To our knowledge, this would be the last investigation at the Diamonds.

In October 2007, I was working at the New Haven Police Station when a man came in to see me. He was wearing a handkerchief over his hair with the image of a skull on it. His arms were covered in jailhouse tattoos, including the words 'pure hate' on his fingers spelled out just above the knuckles. It was obvious he was uncomfortable speaking with the police.

"Uh, . . . the guys in the bait shop said you'd want to hear my ghost story," Stephen Miller said. "I know about the ghosts in Tri-County."

Stephen's tale, while intriguing, had to be censored considerably due to his colorful prison language. The changes have the same basic meaning, but with socially-acceptable adjectives.

Miller told his story. Because windows had been broken out of the closed restaurant, his brother, Kevin, had been hired to work security at the Tri-County Truck Stop. Kevin Miller was living in a small trailer on the premises. Kevin and Stephen, along with another brother, had worked there through much of the late 80's and 90's, and even into the 21st century.

Stephen Miller remembered George, whom he describes as the "ghost in the bathroom." He is not afraid of George. Stephen says George used to open the bathroom door while he was in there.

Miller read the original story of the ghost investigation while he was in the slammer and had remarked to his friends that he knew of George, but he was unprepared for the other spirit.

"I was talking to Kevin, and he was talking about the ghost upstairs. I told him, 'I ain't no coward! I'll go in.' "

Kevin, who was also working on cleaning up the interior, opened the door for his brother but stayed outside. "I was going to ask what he was doing, when we heard a voice say 'Get Out!' I told him there was someone in there, and started to run in to find whoever it was. But Kevin didn't move. He told me there wasn't any one in there."

Stephen searched the downstairs, finding no one. His brother remained on the restaurant floor. Kevin told his brother that he was not afraid of the child ghost, who followed him around while he worked, nor of George, who he knew was the ghost there since he first worked there more than a decade earlier. But he was not going upstairs or in the basement.

Stephen said he went upstairs and opened a door, turning the knob and pushing in. The door suddenly pushed against him, shutting. Stephen forced the door open approximately two feet, when it was slammed on him again, pushing him backwards into the office. Stephen left the area.

Later, Stephen said he went back with his wife and nephew, who didn't believe either. As he walked up the steps, his wife stopped him with a shushing noise. He could then hear the footsteps on the stairs, as the ghost seemed to walk past him. He checked the building for others inside, finding no one.

Once upstairs, Stephen said he entered the main room where he could see the chairs had been left in a semi-circle from our last trip there. He turned to show his family the door that had slammed on him, and when they turned back around, an old office chair on a swivel base had turned to face them. All of them knew the chair had been facing the same direction as the others.

Suddenly, a door slammed shut. Stephen looked around to find his family had deserted him in great haste. He left also.

Once outside, his brother broke even bigger news to him. As his family retreated, the ground outside seemed to shake. Stephen said he would not return upstairs.

His brother needed the back door locked. Stephen agreed to do so, saying again "I ain't no coward." But as he walked up to the door, Stephen paused…

"What happened?" I asked.

Stephen, who has faced the fear of the courtroom and the horrors of prison, took a deep breath before answering.

"The voice again told me to 'Get Out!' I locked the inside doorknob and slammed it behind me." Stephen was visibly shaken from relating the story, even showing me the gooseflesh that had risen on his arms from the memory.

Tina Frank worked at the Tri-County Truck Stop from 1996 to 1999. The spirits introduced themselves immediately. "About two weeks after I started," Tina told me, "I was stocking those large, commercial-sized cans of vegetables in the pantry. The manager then had a marked place for each type, and I put them in the right place.

"I left the pantry to get some other things. I was only gone a few minutes but when I returned, the cans were all mixed up!"

Tina worked the breakfast buffet. "Anything hot on the buffet was fine," she said. "But the cold stuff would get moved to other positions, and sometimes just spread around the counter. The ghosts were just playing."

"Breaks were scheduled but I'd still wait until someone else went into the bathroom before I'd go in. It was just spooky! And if the other person left, I'd hurry up and leave."

When I made a comment about the basement, Tina was quick to reply. "I hated that place. If we wanted to smoke inside, we had to go down there. Once, some of the boys working there locked me in, and I felt something grab my arm and squeeze it as I pounded on the door. I never went down there again!"

Another former employee, Daniel Hogue, recalled he had worked for the Tri-County Truck Stop in the mid 90's. While working on a hot water heater in the basement, he said he had to work standing next to the controls, rather than in front of them. "I just couldn't stand to have my back to the basement." he said.

Once, while working in the kitchen, Dan heard a noise in the upstairs section. He and another employee checked the stairs where, according to Dan, a large child's ball bounced down the stairs, accompanied by the childish laughter of what he believed to be a little girl. The two employees checked upstairs, finding no one. I asked if the ball had disappeared and Dan looked surprised. "No, it was still there when we went back downstairs. I threw it back up, so they could play." Dan quit the job a few weeks later. Kevin also quit working there.

The fate of the old building is uncertain. One thing is for certain. The time for the Diamonds has past. The age of cheap gas, long trips, and an oasis of civilization after miles of lonely Route 66 has passed into history. But some of the travelers on that long-gone, dusty trail remain behind at the old Tri-County Truck Stop, waiting for someone to tell their story. And here it is. . . .

Photo by Dan Terry

***Sherri Terry and Tim Clifton challenge ghosts** at Tri-County Restaurant, formerly the Old Diamonds at Gray Summit, Missouri. Clifton had called to the ghosts of the murdered woman and child not to be afraid, then he began challenging the ghost of the murderer to come out. Three orbs appeared above him that were not present in photographs that had been taken a few minutes earlier. Clifton was formerly an investigator with Missouri Paranormal Research and is also a Baptist minister.*

XANDER: *Oh, no, no. No. No cool. This was no wimpy chain rattler. This was, "I'm dead as hell, and I'm not gonna take it anymore.*

—Buffy, Season Two, "I Only Have Eyes For You."

Photo by Dan Terry

The remains of an old building at Blackwell, Misouri, *which is, reportedly, haunted by a ghostly nun, whom local legend says was murdered in 1862. A young girl was also, reportedly, raped and murdered at the site. A hanging took place near this building. EVP readings provided evidence of paranormal activity. Investigators were able to make contact with the spirit.*

St. Francois County, Missouri

Chapter 7

History and Legends

in Blackwell, it's hard to tell the difference

Blackwell, Missouri has a treasury of urban legends surrounding it. Tales of a restaurant run by human-sacrificing Satan worshippers, phantom couples walking the roads, a raped and murdered nun haunting the scene of her death, and executed soldiers returning to the bridge where they were hanged. One legend involves a disappearing road and a missing Masonic Hall that opened a gateway to Hell.

It's easier to find the legends than the town itself. The first time I tried to locate it, I followed Upper Blackwell Road until I discovered Desoto. Twice. I never found a town.

But Blackwell is more of an area than a town. On my journey there, I located the famous satanic restaurant, abandoned and dilapidated, now situated in a field. The haunted steel bridge, reportedly the scene of a Civil War revenge hanging, has been replaced with one of the new soulless concrete monsters spanning Big River. The Masonic Hall is gone. Stories surrounding the old hall indicate it was moved, brick by brick, because it had been used for conjuring evil spirits, spirits that now roam the area.

After the drive through Blackwell, I gave up on finding ghosts there, at least until March 2008, when fate and Tim Clifton conspired to bring me back.

Tim had called, asking for assistance with a possible demonic infestation. Reportedly, things were being thrown at the residents, who were described as a nice Christian couple. There had always been some activity there, but recently it had turned ugly. The couple had even awakened with bite marks. The most recent occurrence involved the woman being held down in bed where she experienced the sensation of hot water being poured on her back.

This incident, more than any other, flagged it as possibly demonic. As was pointed out to me, this would be the opposite of a baptism, where cool water is poured over the head.

I believe that there is always an invitation of some kind before demonic entities visit. Sometimes demonic entities visit because someone at the site has been using witchcraft or Ouija® boards or living a really bad life. The only other way demonic visitations occur is when you are in a building or site where someone has already invited the demonic in, such as was the case with Steven LaChance and the Union Screaming House. I asked Tim what the invitation was, and he said there was none. When I asked how it got there, he replied, "It's Blackwell."

Blackwell, originally called Blackwell Station, was named for Jeremiah Blackwell, who served as a soldier in the War of 1812 and then settled near Big River. Jeremiah was a farmer and a Mason, as was his son, Aquilia, who lived nearby.

During the Civil War, a skirmish occurred near Blackwell Station in October 1861. Lead ore, which had been mined at Pilot Knob, was being transported by the Iron Mountain Railroad to St. Louis, where it was to be used by the Union for the war effort. Brigadier General M. Jeff Thompson, known as the "Swamp Fox", took his Confederate troops of the 2nd and 3rd Dragoons, Missouri State Guard, to burn the bridge at Blackwell, crippling the supply line and preventing Union troops from moving.

While never a full general, M. Jeff Thompson was treated as one, even by the Union forces after he was captured. General Thompson had been the mayor of St. Joseph, Missouri, from 1857 to 1860, as well as a construction supervisor on the railroad, an investor and a gambler. At the onset of the Civil War, with little or no help from the budget-strapped Confederacy, Thompson raised his own battalion of cavalry, and led them. They became known as the "Swamp Rats". Thompson brought a huge morale boost to the Confederates and to the Missouri Confederate

sympathizers with his raids, bringing early victories to the Southern cause. Using guerilla tactics, his group seized ships and soldiers on the Mississippi River, disappearing into the forest to avoid capture. Thompson was so successful that a ship in the Confederate fleet was named for him. The CSS Gen. M. Jeff Thompson was a sidewheeler known as a "Cotton Clad", due to using bales of cotton to protect against enemy fire.
which used bales of cotton for protection from enemy fire.

The bridge at Blackwell was being guarded by the 33rd Illinois Volunteer Infantry, a unit that had been created by Professor Charles E. Hovey. Professor Hovey had founded a teachers' college in Normal, Illinois, where he served as president. Hovey came up with the idea of creating a unit comprised of the college faculty as officers and college students as soldiers. This unit became known as "Brains" by admirers of the idea, and as "Cracked Brains" by the regular military units. Devoted abolitionists, at one point they took it upon themselves to emancipate slaves in direct disregard of President Lincoln's promise not to free Missouri slaves.

The Swamp Fox, with a cavalry of 500 men, was heading for the bridge, which was being guarded by 40 men of Company E of the 33rd Illinois Volunteers.

In the early morning hours of Tuesday, October 15, Thompson's army attacked from two sides, catching the sleepy, undermanned unit in crossfire. Within ten minutes, the Union force surrendered by waving a white blanket. The Rebel troops quickly looted the camp of food, weapons, powder and any valuables. As was the custom at the time, the Federal troops were paroled upon promising not to fight the Confederacy again. The loss in Federal manpower consisted of one man, Sgt. Foster, killed, and at least seven men wounded. Some of them died later. On the Southern side, two men were killed and two wounded. The bridge was burned.

Another brief battle occurred that day, again won by the overwhelming manpower of the Swamp Fox. By the end of the Battle of Blackwell, total casualties for the Union included one dead, 14 wounded, and 44 captured. Losses suffered by the Confederates included six dead and eight wounded. While this success energized the Southern sympathizers and demoralized the North, the Union army sent a group of Hessians to hold and repair the bridge within weeks. Thompson, instead of following his victories with an attack on Pilot Knob or St. Louis, turned back toward Fredericktown and defeat at the hands of General Ulysses S Grant. It would be three years before any Southern unit got that close to St. Louis again.

According to local legend, several Union soldiers, along with people who had helped them, were hanged from the steel bridge near the scene of the battle. This cannot be confirmed because many of the soldiers who had been paroled just went home. According to an article in the October 13, 2007 issue of the *St. Louis Post Dispatch,* at least 33 Union troops were listed as missing in that battle.

What is known is that revenge killings occurred all over Missouri between the factions. As reported in the book, *The Battle of Blackwell,* by local historian John Hollingsworth, local history from three separate oral sources recorded shortly after the war tell the tale of the Crucified Confederate.

According to Hollingsworth, Union troops, enraged at the defeat, tracked down and harassed Southern sympathizers. They captured a Southern sympathizer in Blackwell who had, reportedly, been seen at the site of the bridge. Laying him spread eagle on a railroad flat car, they nailed his hands and feet down to the floor of the car, tortured him with hot wax, then transported him to DeSoto. Upon reaching DeSoto, he was dragged down the street behind a horse, then his dead body was hanged on a tree overlooking the town. They had hoped to use the body swinging above DeSoto as a warning to other sympathizers; however, the man's family cut the body down and buried it during the night.

Another incident reported resulted in a court trial. On August 22, 1862, James Edmonds entered the house of R. D. Massey, reportedly looking for militia men who might be hiding there. Finding only a group of women, Edmonds decided to have one of them. A partner, identified only as Conrad, tried to stop him and Edmonds fired a fatal shot at him.

Margret Massey, being "12 years of age and upwards" according to the court record, was "forced to accompany" Edmonds outside for some three hours. Edmonds was charged with rape and murder. He was sentenced on March 3, 1863, to be " Hung by the Neck until Dead, Dead, Dead!"

Edmonds was buried in Hillsboro.

Is Blackwell haunted by the spirits of its past? Even Hollingsworth, whose book is purely historical, if somewhat one-sided, mentions in the epilogue that Blackwell has "a peculiar feel to it."

Tim and Steven thought I would like to go with them to Blackwell for an investigation so Sherri and I accompanied Theresa, Steven, Tim, and Tim's daughter, Ginny, there. I took some preliminary photos, and while waiting for the sun to go down, Tim, Sherri, Ginny and I went to the location of the former hanging bridge for an impromptu investigation. We were advised by the victims to check out the burned-out building near the tracks as it was said to be haunted by a ghostly nun.

After checking out the bridge area, we went to the old basement. The presence of an old, rusty safe with no door lying on its side indicated this had been a business of some type. Small trees and high weeds growing among the charred timbers indicated the amount of time since a building had stood on the old basement. Nestled against a hill, we could see an old shed or pump house, where a water pump stood sentry over the old well, just outside the scorched concrete walls.

Tim and I stepped inside the concrete basement while Sherri and Ginny checked the outbuildings. As I took photos, I noticed a shadow person move from behind a tree into the shed. When I pointed this out to Tim, he said we weren't alone.

Tim began asking questions, attempting to get an EVP. I continued to photograph. I kept hearing what I believed to be footsteps in the snow, as if something was breaking though a layer of hard, crusty snow and ice. However, the snow was fresh.

Suddenly, Tim asked if I saw anything walking the wall. He believed he had seen something walking, not something of substance, but almost like light was bending around it. He compared what he had seen to light waves coming off hot pavement in the distance.

Watching for a while, I saw it also. There was a shimmering effect to it as it moved. Tim continued to ask questions.

I then saw a thin weed, standing about four foot tall, moving back and forth. None of the other weeds, most of which were equally tall or more, moved. Neither did the trees. That one small weed shook violently after certain questions.

I pointed this out to Tim. That plant stopped moving but another one a couple of feet away began. When Tim asked if the spirit here was moving the plant, it began to shake even more.

Tim asked for a sound. At that moment, I heard what sounded like a male produce a loud and extended sigh. There was a guttural overtone, as if he were trying to be heard. I asked if anyone else heard that. Everyone had. Tim continued to ask questions, and the weed, completely surrounded by high concrete walls, continued to shake in response.

Eventually, it stopped responding. I asked for a sign that it was still there and the snow on a small cedar tree next to me fell from the top without reason. A later check of EVP's showed some speaking, most of which could not be understood. The heavy sigh was recorded as was our surprised response.

We returned to the house. The family involved, wishing to maintain their anonymity, will be referred to as Bob and Patty.

Patty said there had been several small episodes but never anything harmful. Recently, however, she had noticed a number of shadow people moving around in the woods, staying just within the tree line. She had felt uncomfortable using her own hot tub and back porch area.

One of her children, experimenting with the gothic lifestyle, began hanging around the cemeteries. One old Masonic cemetery was, reportedly, quite haunted. Patty believed that her child had been performing some kind of ritual there. It was after the visit to the cemetery that things became more active. Now we had discovered the invitation.

As we were given a tour of the home, I saw the human-shaped darkness of a shadow person step behind a tall vase in the bedroom. Psychics Theresa Reavey and Tim Clifton both felt a presence there although it could not be identified. Theresa believed the spirit was human and described him.

Patty had called in a paranormal investigation team from the St. Louis area. While explaining this, Patty described the team as "a bunch of housewives playing ghost hunter." After some investigation at the home, they had insisted that Patty take them to the Masonic cemetery.

Once there, Patty stepped over a grave, suddenly finding herself extremely dizzy and falling to the ground. LaChance believes this is when the spirit attached itself to her.

The St. Louis group had looked at the evidence—bite marks, things being thrown around the room, and feelings of dread and fear. They then insisted that Patty was simply being visited by a much-loved relative who had passed on, and she was not in any danger.

This is a case where a group, representing themselves as professionals, had no inclination of what was going on, made a situation worse, and then abandoned the victims. Patty said she had tried to contact them when the spirit became more violent, but they would not return her calls.

I set up a video camera in an extra bedroom, then assisted Tim with an EVP session in the bedroom. There we found that something was affecting Tim's digital thermometer. Although there were new batteries in it, it gave strange readings showing temperature changes of 20 to 30 degrees over distances of only a few feet. Ginny believed she had been touched repeatedly by an unearthly hand. Both Tim and his daughter, who is also psychic, heard voices inside the bedroom. One, a male voice, answered the question of why they were picking on Patty with the response of "I hate her." Another time, the spirit answered "I can." Ginny heard a female voice saying "She's nice." When Tim asked how long they had been there, both Tim and Ginny heard the answer "Forever". Tim started to answer the spirit's obvious lie, then thought better of it, calling an end to that session.

Ginny, Sherri and I tried an EVP session in the spare bedroom. I was standing in a corner, and suddenly caught the odor of burned electrical wiring. I asked if anyone detected any odors, and Ginny believed she smelled roses. I remained silent about what I believed I had detected, and a few moments later Ginny stated she thought she could smell barbecue, or something burning. When I commented about what I had smelled, she agreed that burning electrical wiring could describe it.

Later, during the stage when we check the evidence, the video camera I had set up in that room showed me going out the door. You can faintly hear Tim and I being given the tour of the house. Then, 17 minutes after the video showed me leaving the room, there was the sound of a voice taking a deep breath, then releasing it, as if disgusted.

Tim and I went outside to try an EVP session. While walking around the house, Tim commented on the beautiful night. With no outside lights to speak of and no nearby cities, the stars shone brightly. Tim made the comment that they must have been very beautiful in the Arctic, knowing I had served on an icebreaker in the U.S. Coast Guard.

He then asked if the lights of the ship interfered. I explained that the lights were put down at night to avoid affecting the night vision of the watch standers on our ships. Later, checking the EVP's, a male voice, at the point where I mentioned "my ship", said "a cruiser?"

We continued around the house. Looking over my shoulder, I saw a shadow person quickly moving across the field from behind the shed to the wood line. Tim wanted the shed photographed in the night, and I obliged. Later, checking the photos, we discovered a white, shapeless blob in the window, and what appeared to be small faces surrounding it. Checking the photos against ones taken earlier in the day, as well as others taken at that time, we found nothing resembling that blob in the window in any other photograph.

Returning inside, we sat with Steven, Patty and Bob while Tim and Theresa prepared for the cleansing. During this time, I continued to photograph the room around us, observing that there was always an orb somewhere in the photo near Patty.

For those skeptics who believe that orbs are always dust or moisture, this is an interesting problem. Patty is the center of the paranormal activity, and in almost every photo of her, an orb is somewhere in the shot. Are we to believe that she failed to bathe, causing dust to constantly spring from her body when the flash went off? I can find no logical reason for the phenomena, except that there was a spirit near her. There was something in this house and it appeared to be attached to Patty.

It was time for the cleansing, or blessing of the house, which is an attempt to drive evil away. Many investigators, either by mistake or to simplify their vocabulary, call this an exorcism. However, most agree that only people can be possessed by the demonic, not homes or property. These are infested by the evil spirits, and must be blessed to break the evil that dwells within. In the case of homes, if the blessing by Tim, a Baptist minister, fails, a stronger or more experienced clergyman must be called in.

One of the stages prior to possession is infestation, followed by oppression. At this point, the demonic entity is playing its evil games, preventing the owners from sleeping, disturbing their appetite and even affecting their economic situation negatively. The games are all cunningly designed to drive them to the brink of exhaustion and frustration, a condition that would allow them to be more susceptible to possession. I believe that Patty had reached the oppression stage.

Surrendering my normal equipment for a video camera, I began recording the blessing. As the head of the household, it was up to Bob to assist Tim by forcefully making the evil spirit leave the residence as Tim prayed, and Theresa followed up the prayer by the expeditious use of holy water.

In another bedroom currently being used as an office, Tim opened the closet door and shuddered. A cool breeze came from the interior and Tim announced that it was inside. As Tim prayed and Theresa sprinkled, something went past us to the hallway outside. Moving into the living room, Tim worked his way to the closet, where once again cool air exited the door. Tim commented that this coward likes closets.

We continued to pursue this thing to the kitchen, where Steven and Patty waited. Tim chased it into the pantry, where I saw Tim suddenly bend at the waist as if kicked. Tim said he believed it was not an attack, but he must have been in the way.

Almost as if by some unspoken signal, Theresa opened the sliding glass door in the kitchen to the outside. Suddenly, Bob perked up, asking in the room if anyone else "felt that?" Steven smiled, looking towards Patty, who was also smiling. The atmosphere in the room seemed lighter, fresher. The oppression was over.

However, the work was not. Tim and I went back outside where he continued to pray and bless the property while Theresa continued to use the holy water and blessed salt to secure the doors.

Soon, the job was over. After nearly 60 days, Patty is still happy and spirit free. The next day, she slept for nearly 16 hours, catching up on the rest she had been denied during her torment.

She's no doubt learned some valuable lessons, including that amateurs and ghost-hunter-wannabees are as dangerous as the spirits they are looking for. But, help is available for anyone who looks for it.

And Blackwell sits on Big River, waiting for the next ghost hunter, or maybe the next victim.

Photo by Dan Terry

Enoch's Knob Bridge, *located off Highway 185 between New Haven and Washington, provides travelers with a spooky route to the other side.*

Franklin County, Missouri

Chapter 8

Crossing into the Twilight Zone

Enoch's Knob Bridge

The bridge stands like a lonely sentry, a rusty steel entrance to another world. Boeuf Creek, depending on the time of year, usually flows below the rusted girders and rotted wooden floor. Its days are numbered. Since the Minnesota bridge collapse, the county has been checking all the bridges, fixing or replacing the worst ones. Bridges of this design are being removed and replaced with newer generic concrete monsters that are safer but have none of the personality.

An internet story led me to the bridge; it was one of the first investigations by Spookstalker. This one described ghosts, demon dogs with glowing eyes, trolls and invisible ghost dogs. It included rumors of heartbroken teenagers hanging themselves off the side, or their bodies being found twisted and broken on the water-covered rocks below.

However, at least in the past 30 years, there have only been two confirmed deaths at the bridge. On August 23, 1987, Patrick Kinneson was attending one of the many parties that took place there nearly every summer weekend. One of the party patrons decided that a nearby cornfield needed a truck to drive through it. The driver got it stuck in the mud and most of the party-goers went to help push his vehicle out of the field, leaving Kinneson behind.

No witnesses were found to explain what happened next. It is believed that Kinneson, who reportedly liked to climb, attempted to scale the rusted girders. Others believe he may have committed suicide, although no one could say why. Either way, Patrick's body was discovered on the rocks below the bridge. In the summer, the water is shallow with rocks sticking out above the surface. Kinneson was pronounced dead at the scene, and the death was ruled accidental.

Friends of Patrick Kinneson say he was a practical joker, and may be to blame for the reports of demon dogs with glowing red eyes, and monsters in the woods. No one has accused the other victim who died there of being funny.

On May 9th, 2005, Stephen Cooksey, 41, met people he called "friends" at the old bridge. The exact purpose of the meeting is believed to have been a drug transaction. Cooksey had an extensive record including forgery and drugs, and he had been charged with narcotics as a prior offender twice. The last charge, dated 2001, put him away for seven years. An overcrowded prison system and good behavior were responsible for him getting out early; he would have been safer behind bars.

Cooksey was killed by multiple shots with a .22 caliber rifle. Left to die, he managed to crawl under his car. The murderers returned and set fire to the vehicle, burning his body as well. Is Cooksey still there in spirit? One county deputy who assisted in the murder investigation related that, while crossing the bridge one night several months later, every electrical device in his car, except the radio, shut off. The engine died and the car continued to coast across the bridge to the other side. Once across the bridge, the electrical devices came back on, and he was able to start the engine with no trouble. That deputy said he would not do routine patrol across the devil's bridge again.

I've been out to the bridge on numerous occasions, sometimes alone, sometimes with a group. Frank Garren and I investigated twice, once in the daytime and once at night. The nighttime investigation got nothing. The daytime trip was more fruitful. Frank got a photo of what appears to be a whirlwind on the far side of the bridge. On the day we were there, there was no wind or whirlwinds when the photo was taken. This is consistent with reports I had often heard of others seeing or photographing whirlwinds on both sides of the bridge. One teenager said he saw a whirlwind come down in the middle of the bridge, touch down and return up like a small tornado into a clear blue sky!

While we were looking at the photo, something that appeared to be a face was seen over the whirlwind location. The human mind sometimes plays tricks, looking for a pattern, some kind of shape in the random dust. So, on this trip, one unexplained whirlwind and a possible face in the dust. Not proof.

On May 13, 2007, I took the two newest members of Spookstalker, Jamie and Loretta, to the bridge for training. When we arrived, I walked to the bridge while Jamie and Loretta checked their cameras and recorders. At that time, their cameras stopped functioning, but the recorders continued. Later, when we checked the recorders, we could hear Jamie complain that the camera had better work, as she would need it the next day. Then, a male voice speaking in a flat, frightening monotone, said "Go to Hell!"

We continued onto the bridge and began the investigation. The atmosphere seemed charged; I knew we weren't alone. At one point, I spread my arms out and said in a loud voice "Ok, Pat. Step over here for a picture! Right here!" At that time, I felt what can only be described as a cobweb touching my hand, a cold and light brushing across the back of my hand. I knew I had been touched; I asked for someone to photograph my hand. This time, Jamie reported that the camera batteries had died. She had just put them in.

Later, while checking the recordings, you can hear my voice saying "Step over for a picture, right here." Then, my voice saying "Someone quick, photograph my hand." During that time, the same monotonous voice as before speaks over my voice a simple question—"Why?"

So, when I asked for him to come over for a photograph, he asked, "Why?", but still came by, brushing my hand. Maybe Pat does have a sense of humor.

At the time, I had decided my investigations were about done at the bridge. However, when my friend, Steven LaChance, contacted me, wanting to return to the bridge on the twentieth anniversary of Pat Kinneson's ill-timed death, I couldn't say no. LaChance is an extreme-haunting survivor and author of the book, *The Uninvited.*

LaChance had been out there several times. He had actually gone to high school with Kinneson. On his last trip to the bridge, he and psychic Theresa Reavey, among others, witnessed shadow people approaching their location. They retreated to the car, which was surrounded by the dark, human-shaped masses. They left as a storm began.

On August 23, 2007, at 11:00 P.M., I met with Loretta and Jamie, along with Steven LaChance, ghost magnet Tim Clifton, Steven's son, whom he identifies as "Matthew" in the story of his own terrifying haunting, and another paranormal group known as the Fly Girls.

From Whiteman Air Force Base, the Fly Girls is made up of female military officers and non-commissioned officers interested in the paranormal. I knew they had assisted MPR with other investigations, but I had never met them. When they arrived, we began the investigation.

Up until then, I had never seen shadow beings outside. That night, however, they were all around. Tim and I walked back to the car for fresh batteries and, upon our return, I saw a shadow climb the north side of the bridge, cross the top, and disappear. Others reported seeing the shadows, and two of the Fly Girls said they observed several such shadow beings while on the way to the bridge.

Tim began acting strange. I continued to photograph but could see Tim struggling. Finally, Tim asked if anyone heard anything unusual. Matthew commented that he thought he heard someone saying "Kinder". Tim replied that he heard someone talking to him in German, and "Kinder", or children, was one of the words he was hearing.

The atmosphere was heavier than I had remembered from previous trips. The Fly Girls were obviously getting nervous, as were the rest of us. Steven was still trying to speak with Kinneson, but was overshadowed by Tim's efforts to discover who was speaking to him.

Jamie was photographing while Tim spoke over the rail of the bridge on the west side. During one flash, I would swear I saw another version of Tim, this time in shadow form, standing next to him. A short time later, Jamie jumped after taking a photograph. She said while looking through the viewfinder of the camera, she took the photo and saw in the flash a red-faced, evil-looking figure standing next to Tim. While the photograph showed only an orb, Jamie was visibly shaken.

A scream broke the night. Long and loud, it echoed across the valley and up the creek. One of the investigators had asked a question, attempting to capture an EVP. Initially, I attributed the scream to a bobcat, but it did seem to come at a questionable time.

The air grew thicker yet. Strangely, I noticed the other side of the bridge, going across the river. While I could see the road behind me, and the cars parked alongside even though it was at least fifty yards away, I could not see the other side of the bridge. A curtain of blackness had descended from the sky and settled in the center of the bridge between us and the other end.

The Fly Girls, with a long drive home ahead of them, were ready to leave. Several of them were obviously nervous. The very atmosphere seemed to bring out feelings of paranoia and fear. Some complained of queasiness in the stomach. As a group, we walked the Fly Girls across the bridge, through the blackness. About halfway across, we could see the other side, but not the side we had just left. Once the other team left the area, we began attempting to get EVP's again.

I was standing near Steven while he attempted to make contact with Kinneson. Steven believed he was in touch with his long-dead friend, and was speaking of old times in high school, old friends and party days. He was relaying messages that Kinneson was upset that some believed he had committed suicide. Steven was attempting to calm his anger, and convince him to move on to another plane.

But while this was going on, my attention was shifted to the show behind me. Tim was now in a full-fledged argument with the ghostly crossing guard, speaking in German. Tim was becoming more and more agitated. The spirit was demanding he come under the bridge, claiming he was a child buried there. Tim was refusing in a most adamant manner. Matthew was also hearing the voice speaking in German. At one point, Tim lost his balance and nearly fell to the floor of the bridge. He said he'd been tripped, as if something had reached up from the wooden base and grabbed him.

As un-psychic as I am, I was even feeling an evil presence here. When Steven decided the night was over, I did not argue. We left the scene of the two tragic deaths, heading for town.

I returned one last time to the bridge in late October, at the request of the newspaper editor from the New Haven Leader. This time, the atmosphere was completely different: calm, quiet and we could see all the way across the bridge with no problems at all. The only odd thing that night was a white mist, which showed up on the editor's digital camera, but not on mine. Since it was an exceptionally warm night for October, we had all noticed the mist on the camera, and checked our breath. It was as invisible as the spirits themselves had been on the last trip.

Up until now, we had never encountered a tree spirit, a glowing-eyed demon, or phantom dogs. What we did encounter is the kind of horror you never see in the movies: unexplained blackness and voices only one or two can hear. A ghost we could all see would have been a comfort. You know you're not crazy if everyone can see it. But voices that are only heard by one or two people can make folks question their sanity. Mind games like this are far more indicative of evil than the image of a knife-wielding, black-robed demon. This is the kind of trap amateur investigators have to watch out for.

I had believed that the whole demon dog story was nonsense. That would change, however, on a cold day in January 2008. I was standing in a local store when approached by an attractive young woman and her husband. She asked if I was the officer who had written the first ghost book, then told me she had photos of the Harney Mansion and a story to tell.

Christine Ransom was a teenager when she went through the Harney Mansion on a ghost tour. It was years ago when the structure was still sound enough to be used for a haunted house for Halloween amusement. One wonders if the people who made the decision had any idea the "haunted mansion" was really a haunted mansion!

At any rate, Christine related to me that while she was walking through the old building, she felt a whisk of a touch across her face. Then something grabbed her ankle, nearly tripping her! When she had seen the photo in my first book of the mist grabbing the ankle of the investigator, it reawakened her memories, and started her on her own ghost adventures.

After leaving the store, Christine and her husband were going out to Enoch's Knob Bridge for their own hunt. A few days later, I received photos of the mansion in the mail and one photo of the bridge with the following explanation:

> *Check out the last picture. This was taken after I talked to you. I was sitting in my Trans Am and my husband got out to take the picture. My car began rocking back and forth and, when he came back, it quit! When I looked at the picture, I had really had enough of the bridge. They look like demon eyes at the bottom of the photo. Two sets of eyes!*

On the photo, I could see two sets of red, glowing eyes in the floor of the bridge. One set was close together, one set larger and farther apart.

Others I have shown the photo to believe they can make out the head of a large dog around the larger set of eyes. This gives the legend of the demon dogs some new evidence. Or, were the eyes another joke by Patrick?

The clerk at a local gas station showed me some photos taken on her trip to the bridge, this time of a white mist. The mist started on the third of three photos, as she approached the bridge on foot. It completely covered the bridge to the point that the steel superstructure was nearly invisible. In the next photo, the mist was completely gone. Other photos showed bright orbs surrounding her and her daughter. The clerk went to get her mother and returned. This time there were no orbs or mist present.

Go to the old bridge if you dare. Honk the horn three times, walk in circles, whatever the internet stories call for to bring a demon dog around. But, try talking to Patrick. If he speaks back in German, run.

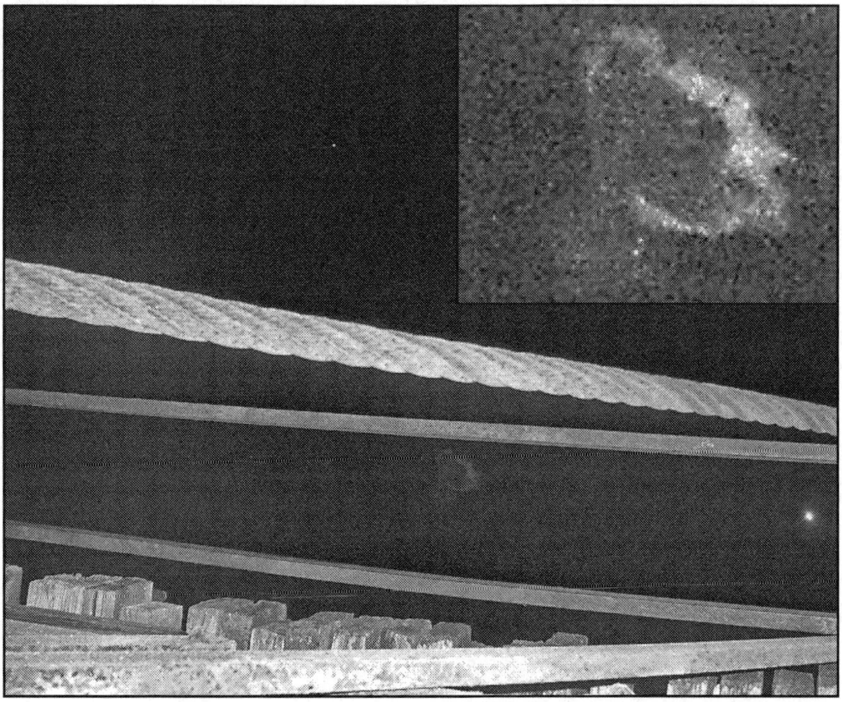

Photo Submitted by Devin Doyle and Scott Sory

One of the demon dogs of Enoch's Knob Bridge *can be seen on this digital photograph. (See enlarged image.)*

Photo by Dan Terry

***The two-story Cooper County Jail** was built in 1848 of limestone blocks quarried by slaves. No prisoners have officially been housed here since the jail closed in 1978, but some have stayed around and frequently make their presence known. The right half of the structure was the jail and the left side, built of brick, served as the sheriff's residence.*

Cooper County, Missouri

Chapter 9

Hung by the Neck Until Dead!

but in the Cooper County Jail, they forgot to tell him he could leave after the execution

In February 1810, Hannah Cole, a widow with nine children, crossed the Missouri River with her brother-in-law, Stephen Cole, his wife, Phoebe, and their five children. They were among the earliest white settlers south of the Missouri River and west of St. Louis. Cousins of Daniel Boone, they set up camp near present-day Boonville. However, they were forced back across the river due to constant attack by the Sac and Fox Indians, as well as the lack of fresh water. They returned a year later, settling near a fort close to the Santa Fe Trail and Missouri River.

Boonville was incorporated in February 1839. The town saw two Civil War battles and was captured during Price's Raid when General Sterling Price came out of Arkansas and, in 1864, wreaked destruction on a path through Missouri. In 1853, the first official Missouri State Fair was held at Boonville. The town continued to grow, and even played host to Thespian Hall, which opened for business in 1857, and has the honor of being the oldest theater still in use west of the Allegheny Mountains.

Photo by Dan Terry

A glimpse of a cell in the Cooper County Jail. *The windowless, coffin-sized steel cells housed prisoners for over 100 years. Could some have chosen to stay in the cold, damp boxes?*

As any city grows, so does its need for law and order. In 1848, the Cooper County Jail was built at a cost of $6,091.50. Slaves quarried the two-foot thick limestone blocks and transported them for use in building the two-story structure. On the ground level, 1¼ -inch rings were put into the wall for holding chained prisoners as well as slaves bound over until the next auction took place on Main Street.

In 1871, the second floor cells were brought upriver as one piece on the deck of a ship. Using prisoners as labor, the cells were put into place, changing the entire personality of the Cooper County jail system. The steel cells were used to house prisoners for more than 100 years, without any changes being made to the windowless, cold, coffin-sized steel cells.

Also in 1871, a red brick home was built to house the sheriff. It was attached to the limestone jail with one large door opening from the prisoner area to a hallway inside the sheriff's home. Finally, a barn was built to house the sheriff's horses. This stable was later used for executions, and became known as the famous "Cooper County Hanging Barn".

One of the most famous outlaws of Old West fame was once, at least officially, a prisoner there for a very short time. Frank James, brother of slain train robber and murderer Jesse James, was considered a guest of the county even though he was never held in the cells.

Frank James was arrested and transported to Cooper County in 1884 to stand trial for a train robbery in Otterville. Sheriff John Rogers brought the famous Wild West outlaw into the office, where he was booked. Then Sheriff Rogers took Frank, not to the cells, but out the back door to the city hotel for supper. During his short stay in Boonville, several local businessmen came up with bond money, and the notorious murderer, robber and ex-Confederate irregular was released that same night.

Frank James returned to stand trial in Cooper County; however, a former member of the gang, a man who had turned state's evidence and had expressed willingness to testify against Frank James, could not be found. He had disappeared. Charges against Frank James were dropped for lack of evidence.

Until the 1960's the first floor was open with rings on the walls for chaining prisoners. Installing cells was the last major change until 1978, when the jail was forced to close after a federal court declared imprisonment there to be cruel and unusual punishment in response to a lawsuit filed by a prisoner. Its closing marked the end of Boonville's

Photo by Dan Terry

***A noose still hangs inside the Hanging Barn** in Cooper County as a grim reminder of the fate that awaited at least six prisoners who were once housed in the Cooper County Jail.*

distinction of having the oldest continuously-used county jail in Missouri.

On March 14, 2008, I went to the jail looking for ghosts. I was attracted to it because of the "hanging barn", and the limestone block walls. Limestone has long been associated with ghosts.

Approaching the building, you can see that the red brick of the sheriff's home clashes with the older, stone-colored limestone blocks of the older jail section. Two red, white and blue welcome flags beckon visitors to the older home.

Once inside, I met with an employee of Friends of Historic Boonville, the organization that currently owns the building. When I explained that I was looking for information on a possible haunting, the employee was ready to talk about it. Apparently, there were quite a few stories to tell about the historic jail, involving moving mists, strange sounds and ghostly handprints.

The employee was convinced the jail section is haunted. The guide spoke of feelings of being watched. At other times, the sound of people descending the stairs with no one in the building echoes through the halls. Recently, a paranormal group was allowed to investigate the jail. Psychics with them believed there were several spirits, including that of a young man. Visitors also have reported feelings of dread, or of being watched.

My host opened the large steel door separating the offices and residence from the jail. Stepping inside, I felt the temperature immediately drop by what felt like 30 degrees. This temperature drop was not paranormal in source, but rather the natural ability of the huge limestone blocks to hold the cool air. Inside, the cells brought back memories of the 1970's movies of Southern county jails with the paint peeling off the bars and cold steel beds hanging from the walls. Graffiti on the walls attested to years of housing unwilling guests. Stark, cold, but livable. I mentioned to my guide that I could not understand what made this specifically bad enough for the federal court to close it. No, it was not the Hilton, but if a criminal wanted comfort, stop breaking the law.

I went up the rickety steps, concerned that I could fall through. Upon reaching the top, I suddenly understood why it was closed. As a career police officer with little soft feelings toward criminals, I can testify that I wouldn't let Charles Manson live in a steel hell like this!

The first cell was a steel box with a door less than five feet high. Inside the room there were no windows, no light, no source of flowing air, no bed, no water or toilet facilities. In this room, Lawrence Mabry spent the last two years of an incredibly short life waiting in the dank, cold dark for a hangman's noose.

Larry was 17 when he made a mistake. He and another man were accused of a robbery and murder, which had occurred during a holdup in Sedalia. Mabry was convicted of the murder based on the story of his criminal partner, who had managed to save his own neck from the gallows, even though the boy said he was innocent of the murder. He was, by order of the court, to be taken out back and "hung by the neck until dead."

In January 1930, Larry Mabry was brought from the second floor of the jail, escorted down the steps and out the back to the hanging barn. The sides of the barn were open, and 50 people had gathered there for the night's entertainment.

Once inside the barn, Mabry was walked up the 13 wooden steps to the hayloft. After a short prayer, the trapdoor was sprung. Lawrence Mabry died instantly of a broken neck while an audience of 50 saw him kick his last. He proclaimed his innocence to the very end.

As a final gesture of contempt, the body was cut down and handed directly to his mother and sister, without the courtesy of a coffin or bag. This was the last public hanging in Missouri.

At least five other hangings took place on the gallows in the yard or barn between 1875 and 1930. One hanging occurred not at the jail, but down the street in Boonville, in the late 1870's.

John West, after being convicted of murder in Cooper County, was taken from the jail and forced to ride in a wagon while sitting on his own coffin. He was driven to the end of Morgan Street, where he was hanged from a tree in what turned into a major social event, with more than a thousand people bringing picnic lunches to enjoy the show.

John Oscar Turlington had been arrested on a minor assault charge and was being held at the Cooper County Jail. Sheriff Thomas C. Cramner went to check on his prisoner, not knowing that a recent visitor from Sedalia has passed a small revolver to Turlington. The sheriff was shot and killed inside the jail.

Turlington managed to escape but was recaptured three days later. It was then discovered that the prisoner who was being held for simple assault was also wanted for murder and train robbery.

He was indicted for the murder of the sheriff but managed

Photo by Dan Terry

The Cooper County Jail Barn *once served as a stable and carriage house for the Cooper County Jail. The barn was the site of several hangings.*

to escape on two more occasions. His second escape was managed by placing a dummy in his bed and getting out of the cell by undiscovered means. That time, Turlington was found in Kentucky and returned. On December 21, 1890, Turlington managed to cut a cell bar with a hidden saw blade and escaped a third time. He had stolen the sheriff's horse and made his getaway, but was recaptured in Otterville, Missouri, where he spent a long and sleepless night in the jail surrounded by a lynch mob. As was reported in the December 22, 1890 issue of the New York Times:

> *. . . and it is altogether probable that he will be lynched before morning. At 10 o'clock tonight, the jail in Otterville is surrounded by a mob. Otterville was the home of Sheriff Cramner.*

But John Turlington managed to avoid being lynched, only to be hanged on March 6, 1891 at age 26. Could his spirit, or that of his victim, still be waiting at the Cooper County jail?

Local legend tells us of an incident that occurred in the late sixties or early seventies. A young man, approximately 26, died in one of the cells while in legal custody. While suicide is hinted at by local sources, it is unlikely because the fact that he was found dead in his cell was all that had been notated in the report.

Was Mabry, or West, or one of the other men who died there, the same man the psychic felt upstairs? And who is making the workers there aware that he's around, seen or unseen?

Employees related several other paranormal stories. A few weeks before my visit, a very large set of handprints were on the inside window of an office, as if someone had attempted to open the window. none of the employees who have access to the room have hands nearly that big.

The week prior to my visit, one employee reported hearing a noise while closing up for the day. The only other living person present denied having made the noise.

Just then a banging noise was heard. The reporting employee, who prefers to remain nameless, said it sounded like a heavy ball had been rolled down the steps from the upper cells to the lower cell area, striking each step on the way down. After a quick check, which confirmed that nothing there could have made that noise, the decision was made to bring in the flags and leave. As my source stepped outside, the porch light suddenly came on by itself! The switch was inside the house, flipped on by unseen hands. The flags were put away and the employee quickly left, holding off telling other employees for several days, to avoid causing anyone to panic. However, my presence seemed a good time to let the cat out of the bag.

I took some photos at the jail office and obtained a few orbs—nothing earth shattering. Still, with a history like this, combined with the reports of activity, there must be at least one spirit there. Could he be waiting for a pardon, or parole? Or revenge? Obviously, execution wasn't enough.

Judge for yourself its believability, and then try to tell yourself, wherever you may be, it couldn't happen here.

—Carl Kolchak

Photo by Nick Corey of Jasper Haunts

The Joplin Spook Light *has mystified area residents and visitors for many years. Could the phenomenon simply be caused by a miner, dead for 130 years, searching for his family?*

Newton County, Missouri

Chapter 10

Swamp Gas

a host of legends and theories cannot explain the Joplin Spook Light

The train stopped at Maco, North Carolina on its trip through the Coastal South. A railroad employee, carrying a green lantern, walked down the tracks on an inspection. Noticing the unusual green light, a rail passenger, President Grover Cleveland asked about the color.

A porter answered him. "That's to distinguish him from Joe Baldwin, Mr. President."

The porter relayed the story. In 1867, a conductor on the train making the run from Wilmington, North Carolina to Georgia, discovered the last car of the train, the one he was in, had become disconnected and was moving backwards. Aware that a fast-moving train was behind them, Joe made his way to the rear of the car, and began frantically waving his light back and forth, trying to warn the approaching train.

In the collision, Joe Baldwin was decapitated. Since then, a glowing light has been seen bouncing around the tracks, and most believe it is Joe looking for his head. Anyone walking the tracks now carries a different color light so that they can be recognized.

Satisfied, the President returned to his car. The legend of the headless conductor continued, and today, near Wilmington, a housing development has been named for Joe Baldwin.

Spook lights have been reported in many states and several other countries, from the Marfa Lights in Texas, the Taos Lights near Taos, New Mexico, Surrency Lights in Georgia, Washington Township Lights in New Jersey, to the Bodhisattva Lights in the Western mountains of China. Most don't have an American President to bring the story to the nation's forefront, but are at least locally famous. And one of the most famous of these is the Joplin Spooklight.

First encountered in 1836, during the forced, traumatic westward exodus of the Cherokee Indian tribes known as the Trail of Tears, the spooklight received its first official notice in 1881, in the publication of *Ozark Spooklight* by Foster Young. In 1896, the small town of Hornet was blasted by encounters with the light, floating across the fields, between the cattle with no reaction from them. Originally seen in Missouri, the light is most often in Oklahoma, although it appears to be best seen from the Missouri side of the border.

Unlike the Maco light, with one story of origin, there are several legends about the Hornet spooklight. The Quapaw Indian tribe, which lived nearby, told early witnesses a tale of two young lovers, forbidden to marry by the chief. The lovestruck couple attempted to elope, and was hunted down by a tribal hunting party. The couple, to avoid capture, jumped from a bluff to their death, and are together forever in the afterlife.

From the 1870's, a legend surfaced of a miner whose cabin had been raided by Indians, his wife and child taken as prisoners. When the miner returned and found his family gone, he began searching, using a lantern to try to find the trail. Even after death, he continues his search. Lastly, a farmer who was captured and beheaded by hostile Indians, continues to search for his head in the area.

Researchers from far and wide have come to the lonely corner of Western Newton County in search of the truth behind the famous spooklight. The first recorded investigation was in 1942 by a group of students from a university in Michigan. The students and instructors observed the light, searched for foxfire, a glow given off by some decaying vegetation, swamp gas, lights from cars or homes, and found no explanation. Reportedly, several of the students even fired at the light with high-powered rifles. The light blinked, but returned unaltered. No explanation was found.

In 1946, the Army Corps of Engineers began a study of the light. They attempted to prove that the lights were the result of automobile lights several miles away. No explanation was given as to how the lights got there, moved around cattle, or where they might have come from in 1881. Again, no conclusion.

In 1955, a group of students from the Shawnee Mission High School in Shawnee Mission, Kansas, again tried, with the same results. In 1965, *Popular Mechanics* sent a team in and they came to the conclusion that it was not atmospheric in nature, but probably billboard lights or lights from the highway. Again, which lighted billboards were up in 1881?

It is known as the Devil's Promenade, the Hornet Spooklight, the Joplin Spooklight, or the Tri-State Spooklight. Numerous paranormal groups as well as UFO research teams have investigated, all with no luck. Troy Taylor, paranormal investigator and author, takes regular tours down to see the spooklight, and is seldom disappointed.

Nick Corey is an author and the founder of Jasper Haunts, a paranormal research group located in Joplin, Missouri. His interest in the Spooklight comes from a very personal experience.

"I was about five years old," Nick explained. "My dad used to take us kids out to see the spook light. For us, it was like a night at the movie. My dad was into the spooky stuff."

Nick's parents, a friend of his father, and his children went out to see the lights. "There were about eight of us crowded into the station wagon, and we were heading for the bleachers that used to be set up for people to sit on while they watched the light.

"Suddenly, a ball of light, the size of a cantaloupe, came from the road in front of us, zoomed through the windshield and stopped in the middle of the car, just sitting there. Then, it beamed back out of the windshield, following its original trail, and was gone."

Nick has seen the light multiple times since those early years and, since forming Japer Haunts, has investigated it three times. He's taken photos of the light, seen it change color, and even believes he's seen and heard something walking around in the woods near the area of the light. He described a tall, thin being with a scaly type of skin, rather like a bigfoot-type creature.

The investigations continue in the region. Whether you believe it is swamp gas, foxfire, headlights, or miners searching for their heads, the light does exist. Visit and make up your own mind.

Photo by Dan Terry

The Jackson County Jail at Independence has held a variety of prisoners. In 1859, the newest jail was built with slave labor on the site of an original log and stone jail. Each cell had one small window and one potbellied stove on each floor provided the only heat source.

Jackson County, Missouri

Chapter 11

Equal Opportunity Jail

police, civilians, Mormons, preachers and famous outlaws resided in the Jackson County Jail

Jackson County was officially established on December 15, 1826. That year, the Missouri General Assembly organized and named the area for the seventh American president, Andrew Jackson. The land itself was not originally part of Missouri, but had been purchased earlier that year at a cost of $800.

Prior to 1803, only Indians and fur trappers had occupied this area. In 1803, according to the journals of the Lewis and Clark expedition, the party stopped to pick wild apples, raspberries, and plums, in the area now known as Independence. Nearby, an area settled by the Kanza Indians would forever carry their name, Kansas City.

In 1821, the year Missouri was recognized as a state, Francois Chouteau, a French fur trader, set out from St. Louis to make his fortune. Chouteau started the American Fur Company where the Kaw River runs into the Missouri River. A flood destroyed the base, and Chouteau moved on to the Independence area.

The town of Independence was officially incorporated on October 13, 1884. Already a bustling town, the city was considered a starting point on the Santa Fe, California and Oregon trails. Beginning in 1841, it is estimated that within the first 20 years, some 300,000 pioneers passed through Independence on the Oregon Trail alone.

Today, Independence sits in the shadow of Kansas City. It is a town that remembers its past, evident with the rebuilt 1933 courtroom and offices of then Judge Harry Truman, destined to become the President of the United States. His home also stands today, as well as the original log courthouse, Vaille Mansion, the Chicago-Alton depot, and the 1859 Jail and Marshal's home.

The first jail for the City of Independence was built in 1827 of log and stone. As was fitting for the time, the jail came complete with a dungeon, which was put to good use in 1833 when a mob decided to lynch the local Mormon leaders. A.S. Gilbert, Isaac Morley, John Corrill, and W.E. McLellin were hidden from the angry mob in the dungeon until they could be smuggled out under cover of darkness.

In the late 1830's, Henry Gastar, being held for the shooting death of one Williamson Hawkins over the matter of $150.00, and Alpha Buckley who, while intoxicated, crushed William Yocum's skull with a rock, managed to tunnel out of the jail to freedom. It was temporary freedom for Gastar, who was found in Southwest Missouri and recaptured. Sent back to Independence, Gastar was hung for murder on March 10, 1839 in the first legal hanging in Jackson County. Buckley was never found.

The story of the first jail would end in 1840, when a neighbor emptied her hot stove ashes outside against the stone foundation. The logs caught fire, and the first jail burned to the ground.

A new brick jail was built in 1841, heralded to be "Escape Proof". Naturally, two prisoners promptly escaped, one by cutting a hole in the east wall, the other cutting a hole in the door, reaching through and unlocking it. The other interesting historical tidbit occurred in 1845. Written in the book *History of the 1859 Jail* by Donald Hale and Vicki P. Beck, a young attorney named George Harper, jealous over the attention his wife was giving a boarder named Owen Merdith, invited Merdith into the parlor for a game of cards. A short time later, a shot rang out and Merdith was killed, reportedly after accusing Harper of cheating him and attempting to pull his own gun. Harper was jailed, and his wife would visit him daily.

One day, Mrs. Harper came to visit her husband, wearing a large dress and a huge hat. The sheriff, accustomed to her visits, allowed her to go inside unescorted. A short time later, she left. The next morning, as the jailer was handing out the morning meal, he noticed the hands of the prisoner were somewhat feminine. Opening the cell door, it was discovered that Harper had switched clothes with his wife the day before, and made his escape.

Because Mrs. Harper came from an influential family, no charges were pressed against her. George Harper was recaptured in 1847, returned to the jail, and later acquitted of the murder charge due to lack of evidence.

In 1859, the newest jail was built on the site of the original log and stone jail. Using slave labor, the massive limestone blocks were hand-fitted into place, forming a two-story jail with a total of 12 cells. Each cell held one small window, and one potbellied stove on each floor served as the only source of heat in the cold Missouri winters.

A two-story brick addition was used to house the county marshal and his family. The marshal received his home and $35. per month. The marshal's wife also received a few dollars a month to cook for the prisoners.

On December 10, 1860, William Clark Quantrill was held temporarily in this jail, though more as a hero than a criminal. He soon became the leader of the infamous Confederate raiding group known as Quantrill's Irregulars, whose members included such notable outlaws as Frank and Jesse James, and Bob and Cole Younger. Quantrill had led a group of abolitionists from Lawrence, KS on a slave-stealing and rescue raid. Quantrill had already informed the ranch owner of the attempted rescue, and he was waiting with five men in an ambush. Two of the would-be rescuers were killed and two more wounded, while one escaped. The wounded were hunted down and killed, buried where they fell in unmarked graves. Due to rumors of a revenge lynching, Quantrill was held in the jail until nightfall, when he was moved to a local hotel and eventually to freedom.

This would not be the only dealings the Rebel leader would have with the Jackson County Jail. Harrison Trow, one of the raiders and friend to future outlaw Jesse James, was captured and brought to the jail. During his time there, Trow was chained down to the floor and tormented by one of the jailers. Eventually, Trow escaped and rejoined the raiders, but an intense hatred had been fueled toward the city marshal and his jail.

Marshal Jim Knowles had led and cooperated with Union Col. James T. Buel, helping his 450 Union soldiers into town. On August 11, 1862, the first Battle of Independence occurred when Quantrill attacked with 25 of his own men, and 375 farm boys from the Jackson County area. Another man, Bill Basham, had been identified as one of Quantrill's men and jailed earlier. There is some evidence that, at that time, Basham was not actually a member of Quantrill's Raiders, but did know them.

Also in jail at that time was Marshal Jim Knowles. During an altercation with an intoxicated Irishman, Knowles had killed the drunken man, and was held in jail for murder awaiting the grand jury's decision in the case.

At that time, Quantrill struck, attacking Buel and his men and chasing them all the way to Kansas City. A rescue party went into the jail to rescue Basham and found Marshal Knowles in his cell. George Todd, one of Quantrill's men, identified the marshal and shot him in his cell, leaving him to die on the wrong side of the bars, his life's blood draining onto the cold limestone floor.

Because of the guerrilla activity in the area, the infamous "Order No. 11" was put into effect, to be carried out by Commander Thomas Ewing. Approved by President Lincoln, the order called for the depopulation of four Missouri counties that bordered Kansas and was South of the Missouri River. These counties were Cass, Bates, Jackson, and Vernon.

The order affected the people living in the rural areas, as those living near a handful of cities could stay. Those who could prove their loyalties to the North were allowed to move to the area around these cities but had to leave their family farms. Those who could not prove their allegiance to the Union were forced to leave the area entirely. During this order, the population of Cass County went from 10,000 to less than 700. Crops that were too far from the cities were burned. Closer farms had the crops confiscated for use by the military in the forts, and the owners were paid an unfairly small sum.

Those who had no place to go were jailed. In an effort to make life so miserable that the families would just head east, up to 35 children were placed in cells meant to hold no more than four men. Legend has it that one building used to house women collapsed, killing several young girls.

After the Civil War, the jail was the center of a controversy that

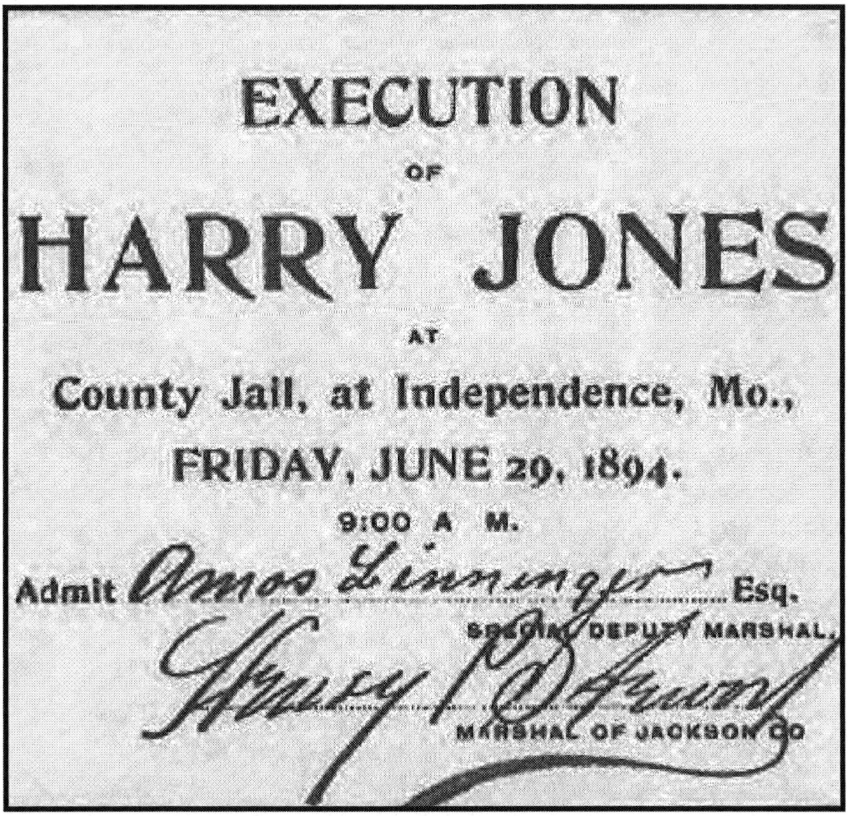

EXECUTION

OF

HARRY JONES

AT

County Jail, at Independence, Mo.,

FRIDAY, JUNE 29, 1894.

9:00 A M.

Admit Amos Linninger Esq.

SPECIAL DEPUTY MARSHAL.

MARSHAL OF JACKSON CO

Tickets to hangings were sold frequently because many people thought it was great entertainment.

would have an effect reaching all the way to the Supreme Court. Rev. A. H. Dean had served with distinction in the Union Army, returning home after the war to resume his church. However, in January 1865, the Missouri state government passed a law that "No person shall be competent as a Bishop, Priest, Deacon, Minister, Elder or other clergymen…" and would not be authorized to "Teach, preach, or solemnize marriages…" without taking an oath of loyalty to the U.S. Government. Rev. Dean refused to take the oath on the grounds that he had never rebelled against his government, adding "My commission to preach comes from the Lord!"

He was in jail for some time. Although the jailers allowed him visitors and personal comforts, life was anything but pleasant behind the limestone walls.

Eventually, public outcry freed the good preacher, and the United States Supreme Court declared the oath requirement unconstitutional.

Another stressful arrest took place in January 1866. Outlaw Cole Younger, former member of Quantrill's Raiders, sent a pistol in for repair. The gunsmith fixed the spring in the grip, without even unloading the pistol. After the repair, 14-year-old John Younger, brother of the outlaw, was sent into town to pick up the weapon.

After retrieving the peacemaker, John stopped off at the local store. There he met up with an Irishman named Gillcreas, bragged about his time with the Union Army. Knowing the child's family and their Confederate sympathies, Gillcreas attempted to start a fight with the younger, smaller boy. When Younger attempted to leave, Gillcreas kicked him hard. That was enough.

John Younger warned Gillcreas, "If you do that again, I'll kill you." Gillcreas kicked the boy still harder, pulling a slingshot out and preparing to shoot it at the boy. However, the boy pulled the pistol he had just picked up from the gunsmith, and fired a single, killing shot into the chest of the bully.

Younger left quickly but was captured and spent time in the county jail. A grand jury eventually decided that the sling shot found in the hand of the body made this an instance of self defense, and John Younger was released. He later joined the famous James-Younger gang, and died in a gunfight against Pinkerton Detectives.

In 1866, another law enforcement officer made the ultimate sacrifice at the Jackson County Jail. Jailer Henry Bugler was living at the house on June 10, when the outlaw Joab Perry was brought in under heavy guard. Perry had ridden with the James Gang, but currently had his own small gang.

On June 13, a group of five men attacked the jail with the intention of freeing Perry. Bugler refused to surrender his prisoner, even when attempts were made to burn down the house his family was in. A gunfight ensued and Bugler was shot and killed. His four-year-old son was also wounded in the fight. The would-be rescuers were forced back, and Joab Perry was brought to trial.

Another of the James gang was housed in Jackson County. Bill Ryan was arrested and convicted for helping the James gang with a train robbery in Glendale, Missouri.

The last chapter of the Old West saga to occur within the limestone walls of the jail began in October 1882, when Frank James, his brother Jesse dead from the gun of a traitor, surrendered himself to Gov. Crittendon. Frank James turned himself in at Jefferson City in Cole County, only to find out that he wasn't wanted there. Instead, he was transferred to Jackson County.

According to the *Independence Sentinel,* "James' trip to Independence was probably one of the most remarkable trips ever witnessed. Great crowds congregated to see the outlaw."

Frank's wife, mother and son met him at the train station and he was allowed time with them. The former Rebel, outlaw, robber, and murderer then had a reception in his honor at the Merchants' Hotel, meeting with some 500 friends and comrades, including some very wealthy, influential people.

As written in the *Rockport Sun,* dated November 22, 1882, "From what we can learn, Frank James is living about as comfortable just now as any feller in the state."

Unlike the other cells, with a single, thin sleeping mat on the cold limestone floor, the cell occupied by Frank James included a Brussells carpet, walls decorated with pictures, and comfortable furniture including a sitting chair and a small but raised bed. The cell door was reportedly unlocked, allowing Frank to have visitors and to see them out as a good host should. One jailer, later fired, took him to the opera house for an evening out. Another let Frank leave at will to get his own tobacco. He was a prisoner, after all.

Local legend says that Frank was eventually moved into the guest bedroom at the marshal's house because the cell was just too cold. Frank was later acquitted of all charges and allowed to return home.

Life continued, with the occasional hanging inside the jail, until February 1920. At that time, the jail was considered too inhumane to be allowed to hold prisoners. It reopened in 1921 because other facilities were overcrowded, but closed permanently in 1933. The jail was used by the Jackson County Welfare League, who had women sewing and canning food for the poor there. In May of 1945, it was given to the local American Legion for a home.

In 1959, the marshal's home was scheduled for demolition. At that time, the Jackson County Historical Society managed to get possession of both parts of the building, and set about restoring it. The later-built cells were removed, and a museum placed there, retaining 12 original cells on two levels. One cell has a small museum inside it which includes makeshift weapons confiscated from prisoners, original firearms and badges of some of the police officers who worked there, as well as some historical relics. Across from that is the Frank James Suite, restored to look similar to when he was a guest of the county.

The other cells contain only a thin sleeping mat on the floor, except for one which has a chain connected to the limestone floor, used to hold exceptionally violent prisoners. The office for the museum is housed in the old prison kitchen where meals were once prepared for the prisoners. Also inside the museum are displays concerning the Civil War in Missouri, clothing and medical equipment of the time, and a one-of-a-kind bar built for Harry Truman.

If you take the time for a tour of the facility, ask for John Ciamciolo as a guide. John has been working at the jail giving tours for 20 years, and has a personal relationship with the jail and the ghost. And John likes to talk about it.

"Right after I started, around January of 1989, the director here then told me people saw curtains move, faces in the windows from outside, and shadows moving in here." John said. "But I'm from Missouri. You know—the 'show me' state. I wanted to see it."

"I've opened up in the morning, along with others, and found photos moved from one wall to another."

Volunteers reported the odor of cigar smoke. "One year," John reported, "we put a small Christmas tree in the Frank James cell. The next morning, we found it sitting right in the middle of the hallway between the cells."

When talking about the center cell on the South side, John visibly shuddered. "In 1992, I came here with some of my family who were in town for a wedding. They were inside the cell where the museum is, and I was standing in the hallway outside in case they had any questions.

"That's when I first saw the shadow person. I heard someone say 'John'. Then, a shadow, a little under six-foot tall, walked out of the main museum, straight towards me. When it got just in front of me, it suddenly turned to the right and walked into the center cell."

Checking inside, John found no one in there. He described it as a shadow, but free-standing rather than on a wall or the floor, as if it were solid. But, he could see through it.

Many believe that this was the cell Marshal Jim Knowles died in. John related another story, this one taking place shortly after he went to work here.

"I was taking this woman through, and she said she was a psychic. She told me there were spirits here, then when she walked by the center cell, she refused to go inside. She did stick her arm inside, and I saw the hair on her arm suddenly stand up!"

Another woman, reportedly psychic, had an experience near the center cell. There was a local group, called a Civil War Roundtable, who met together and discussed the various Civil War battles. They asked to meet here, and talk about the Battle of Lexington, also known as the Battle of the Hemp Bales.

"While walking through the cell area to the museum," John said, "one lady turned white and collapsed into a chair. Her husband rushed to her side and said, "There's a spirit in here." The woman replied "Yes, in the center cell."

When Ciamciolo speaks of his personal relationship with the ghosts, he means personal. One of the spirits sticks with him through thick and thin. "On April 7, 1999, I was going in for heart surgery. I was in the pre-op room, and could not relax. Some doctor I had met for 15 minutes prior to the operation was about to cut me open and mess with my heart!"

"Well, suddenly at the foot of my bed I saw a dark silhouette standing there with an orange glow around it. It nodded yes, and I felt suddenly at ease, like everything was going to be okay. I went right to sleep after that."

Later, complications set in forcing him in March 2000 to go to the Mayo Clinic in Minnesota for further surgery. It happened again, this time in Minnesota. There, at the foot of my bed just before surgery, was the silhouette with the orange glow around it, nodding yes. And again, I fell right to sleep."

But the silhouette is not always so agreeable with John. "In the summer of 2006, I spent a Saturday flying one of my remote control planes at the park. When I was done and driving back home, I decided to come out again the next day, and was deciding which plane to fly."

"Suddenly, in the cab of my pick-up, I smelled cigar smoke. I looked around and saw the black silhouette in my truck! No orange glow this time, and it was violently shaking its head no." John demonstrated how the shadow person was shaking its head. "I wondered what the problem was, then realized I had promised to give two tours of the jail the next day. I had just forgot." The spirit of Jackson County Jail had not.

Volunteers have reported the smell of fresh-baked bread inside the office, which was once the jail kitchen. There are no bakeries within miles of the museum.

Most recently, in March 2007, the ghost of the cell area began to play with John. "The director and I came in because a group was going to use the museum for a meeting. He said he'd get the thermostat going in the marshal's home, and asked me to get the ones in the museum."

"Well, I closed the door to the marshal's home, and went through the cell area to the museum. I turned the thermostat to 72, and watched as it turned itself back to 50 degrees. I turned it back to 72, and it again went back to 50!"

"Once again, I turned it up to 72, and it clicked back down to 50. Then, the door opened to the upstairs. I went back in, shut it again, and returned to the thermostat. This time, the thing was on 72 degrees, right where I wanted it. And I distinctly heard laughing!"

When asked if there were ghosts in the other sections of the museum, John Ciamciolo related a story of a tour in the upstairs of the marshal's home. One psychic stepped into the main bedroom, and suddenly felt ill, breaking into a cold sweat. "And I mean he sweat! We had to get several towels to dry him off."

The first director John worked for also had an experience. "He never would tell me what happened," John related.

"He went upstairs one day, nearly fainted. After that, he

absolutely refused to ever go upstairs again. Never would tell me why."

John is not the only employee who is willing to talk about it. Maryann Noll has worked at the museum for nearly four years, and is usually present when ghost groups investigate.

"I was sitting in the center cell, and it kept getting darker and lighter inside." Maryann related. "I'm kind of a skeptic, I guess. I thought maybe the moon was going in and out behind clouds."

"I walked to the back door," she continued. "I looked out to see the sky, and suddenly I was out on the ground. The first thing I said was 'Who pushed me?' That's what it felt like. Maybe I just fell. But I thought I was pushed."

Maryann also told of a pair of photos, of a man and wife, resting on the wall of the downstairs parlor. Well, maybe "rest" is the wrong word.

"Each morning, the woman's photo was on the floor, leaning against the wall as if it slid down." Maryann reported. "Employees tried tape, wire, larger nails, nothing helped. Every day, it was on the floor."

"Finally, they moved his photo upstairs to separate the pair. The photo has hung in its proper place ever since."

With this history, I had to be there. Spookstalker began an investigation on March 16, 2008. Joining us was Sam Tyree, founder and lead investigator of Great Plains Paranormal Investigations, centered in Wichita, Kansas. We were allowed exclusive access to the entire building from 2:00 P.M. until 10:00 P.M.

With the four-camera DVR (digital video recorder, with infrared night shot) set up in the jail hallway, marshal's bedroom, marshal's office downstairs, and the museum, and another digital camera set up in the child's bedroom, plus a digital voice recorder set up in the center cell, we just waited for darkness to begin the investigation.

As sunset approached, Jamie and Loretta headed upstairs while Sam and I tried the cells. In the center cell, I sat down on the cold floor while Sam videoed the EVP session using his own nightshot camera.

I began speaking to the spirit, introducing myself and Sam, and giving time between each sentence for a response. I seldom got an audible response at the time, but this way of getting EVP, taught to me by Paranormal Task Force Director Greg Myers, has increased the voice captures considerably.

I continued asking questions. I asked if the spirit was that of Marshal Jim Knowles. I then asked for a sound so I knew the spirit was around.

Clink! A loud sound, similar to a quarter being thrown on the floor, came from the corner of the cell near the sleeping mat. I remained quiet. Sam swung the camera towards the sound, then after a few moments of silence asked if I had "heard that?"

I asked what he had heard, and Sam said it sounded like something metallic hitting the stone floor. That confirmed that we had both heard the same noise. Using the flashlight for the first time, we searched the floor of the cell for anything that may have fallen off the wall or ceiling. Nothing was located to explain that noise. I asked for the spirit to do that again, but heard nothing. Shortly after that, Sam mentioned that the cell had a different feeling in it, not as heavy in the air. This is normal when the spirit has left.

During a later review of the evidence, Sam said that as we settled in the center cell, he could hear an EVP with a male voice saying "Get Out."

We then attempted the same in the Frank James Suite. Earlier that day, I had visited Frank's gravesite, letting him know I would be in the cell later and looked forward to hearing from him. Whether he haunts another place or has moved on to his reward, this cell had nothing.

Sam and I then tried the cell directly across from the reportedly most active one. There, I attempted to make contact again, when Sam suddenly stopped me.

"Walk across the cell." he asked. I did so, and he asked me to walk back. "There are orbs all around you. I thought it was dust, but they seemed to follow you."

I then asked if the spirit would like to say anything. As if in response, I felt my right elbow was gently grabbed, as if someone was lightly putting pressure on my elbow, between his thumb and fingers. I asked if he was trying to make contact, and asked that the spirit repeat the move. Again, once was apparently enough.

We moved to another cell, with no response. At that time, Loretta and Jamie returned with a story to tell.

They had attempted an EVP session, even going so far as to lie down on the floor in the area where it is believed Officer Bugler had died. When they moved into another room, trying to make contact with Bugler, Jamie felt a strong pain in the chest.

They rewound the film on the DVR camera in there. It was

obvious where it occurred. Jamie suddenly grabbed her chest, leaned forward, and was walked out. She said that once she was in the hallway, the pain went away.

After a break, Sam and I went upstairs. After an hour of attempted contact, we returned downstairs, where we had a meeting before continuing. I was in the process of sending Jamie back upstairs, this time with Sam, when I glanced over at the computer screen, and saw a large, glowing orb slowly cross in front of the camera in the marshal's office. We checked the office immediately, finding nothing. At that time, there was no detectable air flow in the room.

Jamie attempted to make contact again. Once again, she felt the stabbing pain in the chest, leaving the room after approximately five minutes. Upon their return, Sam and I again attempted to make contact, even daring the spirit to do that to me. Other than a few photos of orbs, I received nothing.

A later check of the evidence showed one very strong EVP, taken downstairs in the jail area. Near the spot where the stairs used to connect both floors of cells, and in the area where at least one hanging reportedly took place, Jamie got an EVP with a male voice chanting in an almost childlike ring-around-the-rosie tune, "My time is o-ver."

While looking for photos for this story, I observed a streak of white down a photo of a Union general hanging in the marshal's office. I thought to myself that I didn't remember seeing that the photo was torn before. Checking other photos, including ones from a similar angle, the lightening bolt-shaped streak never appeared again. I took the photo, along with other photos of the oval-shaped picture, to photography experts who could not give a theory on what caused it.

The Jackson County Jail sits empty at night. At least, empty of the living. A step into the marshal's home is a step into the 19th century. A step into the cell area seems to go back to medieval times, with chains on the floor and the cold, dank walls around the bare, thin sleeping mat. This from a time when jail was punishment, and rehabilitation a word never used in connection with outlaws and rebels. Even today in jail, visitors are welcome. But don't expect the residents to be too talkative.

Photo by Dan Terry

In historic downtown St. Charles, Missouri, *the Mother-in-Law Restaurant is just one of many haunted places. Note the orb in the tree.*

Chapter 12

A Haunted City

downtown St. Charles is a living history lesson . . . and death is no reason for recess

Some places are haunted because of disasters. Some are just historic. Others are haunted because deaths, executions or traumatic events have occurred there. And some are even haunted because the graves of the dead have been molested. But what do you call a place where all of this has occurred?

Haunted Downtown St. Charles!

Walking down the cobblestone streets of downtown St. Charles, you can see yourself going back into history. The quaint shops placed in old homes and buildings, some nearly 200 years old, stand as a living testament to the city's colorful past. There is also a non-living testimony to the past trying to make its presence known.

Because the history of St. Charles is so extensive, it would take an entire book to cover it. The second oldest city west of the Mississippi River, St. Charles was founded in 1765 by explorer Louis Blanchette, who named the area Les Petites Cottes, or The Little Hills. Prior to the Louisiana Purchase, Spanish Lt. Governor Carlos de Hault de Lassus appointed none other than Daniel Boone as the district governor for the Femme Osage District. Boone served until the United States took over the area in 1804. The first church, built in 1791, was dedicated to San Carlos Borromeo.

The log church was built in the Creole style, with the logs placed vertically instead of horizontally. That church was later destroyed but today volunteers are rebuilding it in the original location and style.

St. Charles would provide the last glance at civilization for Lewis and Clark, who left the city for the great, unknown regions of the West.

Several cities competed to house the temporary state capitol until one could be built in Jefferson City. In 1821, St. Charles was selected, largely because a group of businessmen promised the new state government free meeting areas. The state legislature met in a large room above the general store until 1826, when Jefferson City became the new Missouri capital.

The population of Missouri doubled in the 1820's, and had doubled again by 1840. St. Charles became the largest steamboat destination along the Missouri River. Boones Lick Trail, which led to other routes including the Santa Fe Trail, began at St. Charles.

Aside from the extensive history, why does the entire downtown area seem to be haunted?

Around the original church was the church cemetery. In the 1820's, room was needed for the expanding city and the cemetery was moved from Block 28, where the parish had buried its deceased for 40 years, to Block 122 on the other end of the street. In October 1828, Bishop Rosati blessed the new burial ground in Block 122.

At the time, officials said all the graves had been dug up and removed. However, in 1981, excavation near 407 S. Main uncovered what was identified as human bones and remains as well as part of a casket. How many other unfortunates were not moved, possibly buried wrapped only in a blanket due to not having money for a coffin?

It is interesting to note that in 1830, the first graveyard in St. Louis, which was at the present site of the Old Cathedral, was closed for construction and moved. Again, the officials stated that all the graves had been moved. However, a St. Louis undertaker, who had assisted in the removal, later wrote that only bodies claimed by their families had been moved. All the other poor souls were reburied in a mass grave or pit over which the new church was built. Church officials later condemned this story.

Another indicator is the burial of Jean Baptiste Pointe Du Sable.

Du Sable was a Haitian-born explorer and fur trader, who is considered to be the Father of Chicago. It is believed he was born in 1745 to a slave woman and a pirate aboard the ship, Black Sea Gull. Du Sable was educated in France and came to America, where he fought in the Revolutionary War. He later formed a settlement on the North Shore of Lake Michigan just east of the current Michigan Avenue Bridge – a settlement that later became the City of Chicago.

In 1813, Du Sable moved in with a granddaughter in St. Charles, where he died in August 1818. The cemetery was moved to Block 122 and, as the city grew, it was moved again from that area to Randolph St., where it remains today. In the 20th century, when representatives from Chicago wanted to move the body to the city he had founded, the site where Du Sable was supposed to be buried was found to be empty. In fact, legend says that indications were the ground had never even been dug up! One more missing body last known to be buried downtown.

Besides moving the cemetery, a cholera epidemic devastated St. Charles in 1833 as it spread from Europe across the United States. Several hundred people died in the St. Louis area, including St. Charles. Another cholera epidemic hit in 1848 after a ship from New Orleans docked in St. Louis, in which several people had died of cholera while traveling.

Novelist Susan Sontag wrote that cholera was more feared than other deadly diseases because it was so dehumanizing. Diarrhea and dehydration was so severe that the victims literally turned into a "wizened, caricature of his or her former self before death."

Other symptoms of cholera include nausea, dry skin, abdominal cramps, and rapid pulse. It is highly infectious and, without proper treatment, death can occur from 18 hours to several torturous days after initial symptoms appear.

Besides molesting graves and horrible diseases, why is St. Charles so haunted?

On February 26, 1876, a tornado cut a path of destruction and death across the city. At least two children died, along with several adults and city employees. The second story of the jail was completely wrecked and the eight prisoners, while spared, spent a horrifying lifetime inside the fury of the storm.

As was reported in the *Cosmos Extra,* on February 27, 1876:

> *The cells are made wholly from iron, and extend from the floor nearly to the ceiling, in the second story. The walls of this story, on every side, crumbled away, leaving the box-like iron-ribbed cage exposed to view. The inmates, eight in number, were saved from a terrible death by the very bars that shut them out from the world. Waters, the murderer, describes the scene as one of intense horror.*

The prisoners watched as the walls crumbled at their feet and the roof of the building was ripped off and carried over a block away. They had the kind of view that storm chasers would die for.

In the end, more than 20 buildings were destroyed and no downtown buildings were spared from damage. *The Phelps County New Era* reported on March 4, 1876:

> *The heavens were shut out by the debris of wrecked buildings which filled the air so that nothing could be discerned. The roar of the wind was appalling, and everyone was paralyzed by fear.*

In the ruins of the city gas works, the body of James Gosney was found, his son closely clasped in his arms, both bodies mangled beyond description. Another child was last seen being thrown over the Missouri River Bridge, some 90 feet high, his body found later.

Many others were killed and injured.

The old jail sat at the corner of Second Street and Madison. There had been several hangings there, including that of John Bland.

A giant of a man, Bland shot a farmer named Elijah Warren through the window as he lay in bed, nearly decapitating him with a single shotgun blast. Believing to the last that his friends were going to rescue him, Bland was sorely disappointed and attempted an escape while being taken to the gallows. He fought his way from the cell to the outer room, where he was overcome by guards and marched to his death.

A black man named William Barton killed a white man named "Chatterbox" in 1879, just a few months after Bland was hanged. Unlike Bland, Barton met his fate bravely, smiling as the noose was placed over his head.

On June 15, 1905, 250 people, including six women, witnessed the death of Allen Henderson, who had confessed to the shooting and murder of Joe Buckner. He was directed to do so by one of the two men with him. The Henderson house had been set on fire to cover the deed, and his two accomplices were killed before they could go to trial.

Henderson pled guilty, but his plea was refused and the trial commenced. Some believed he was mentally challenged because he never made any attempt at a defense and asked to die. At 10:17 P.M., the trap was sprung, and Henderson fell, but the rope failed to break his neck. Henderson strangled to death, and was pronounced dead some 14 minutes later.

"If I had a thousand lives to lose, I'd die before I'd betray my friends." These were the last words of Bill Jeffries, executed in St. Charles on June 3rd, 1908. Described by the *St. Charles Cosmos-Monitor* as a "game man with the ferocity of a bull dog. His dearest wish was to be permitted to fight Sheriff Hines, whose good detective work hounded him down…" Jeffries, along with his partner, Willis Hood, had murdered dairy farmer William Wussler and escaped. Hood got away but Jeffries had been tracked down by his distinctive shoe print. He never revealed whether he killed Wussler or whether Hood did the deed.

Jeffries' hope was that none of his family would see his execution. His last wish was to be buried next to William Rudolph, famed "Missouri Kid", bank robber and murderer. Rudolph and Jeffries had played together as children and Jeffries believed The Kid to be a fit example to follow.

At 1:45 p.m., the lever was pulled, the trap door opened, and once again the drop failed to break the neck. Jeffries suffered a slow, horrifying death by strangulation, and was pronounced dead some 24 minutes later.

Two final executions are noteworthy. Brothers Andrew and Harry Black, along with Tom Allen, came into St. Charles flashing revolvers, drinking and causing trouble. Officers David Lamb and John Blair, answering complaints about the three, met up with them at the Wabash Depot.

When ordered to throw their hands up, Allen pulled his gun and fired, killing Officer Blair. Lamb returned fire, killing Allen. The Black brothers then began shooting, killing officer Lamb.

Andrew and Harry Black began running, but were captured by a vigilante group in the next town. They surrendered peacefully and were returned to St. Charles.

At the trial, both brothers confessed to shooting at Officer Lamb, claiming self defense. Harry Black testified that he had grabbed the hand of Lamb, in which he held his pistol, and shot Lamb in the head.

After two-and-a-half hours of deliberation, both men were found guilty and the jury recommended death. On August 18, 1916, St. Charles had its first double execution as Harry Black was hanged, his neck breaking immediately, followed twenty minutes later by his brother.

It's not a secret that downtown St. Charles is haunted. The late John Dengler, who owned the Farmers Home building at 700 S. Main Street, spoke of the spirits long before it was fashionable to be haunted.

As reported in the *St. Charles Post* in the October 29, 1997 issue, Dengler and his wife spoke of seeing cigarette packs floating across the room, a voice speaking in French, soothing a crying baby who was also unseen. Other downtown buildings reported in that article include the Mother-in-Law restaurant and the Boones Lick Trail Inn at 1000 S. Main.

The October 14, 1999 issue of the *St. Louis Post-Dispatch* included stories of downtown St. Charles. Ghosts of Confederate officers, French ghosts that hide cigarettes at Dengler's Tobacconist, and a little girl ghost that plays with dolls in one of the stores.

Regrettably, Mr. Dengler passed away in early 2008. The title of St. Charles' ghost expert passed to Dr. Michael Henry.

Author, college instructor, and professional magician, Michael Henry has been running the ghost tours of historic downtown St. Charles for three years. Along with being entertaining, Michael has done the historical research necessary to provide a believable tour of the old city and he was happy to share his research and experiences.

"I've gotten some great photos sent to me by people on the tours," Michael said. "Some, including the ones you took, were so good I couldn't put them on the web site. I was afraid someone would accuse me of using Photoshop or faking them in some way."

Still, Michael Henry considers himself something of a skeptic, especially when it comes to orb photos. But he's certain there are ghosts in St. Charles.

I caught up with Michael while he was between European magic tours. He had just returned from Belfast and was preparing to go to London for another show. When I explained what I was looking for, we spent an afternoon on the back deck of his magic-filled home with a large book containing history, reports of sightings, and personal stories, divided

Photo by Dan Terry

Note the orb in front of this church replica in historical, and haunted, downtown St. Charles.

by addresses.

"The Lady in White is one of the more interesting ghosts seen there," Michael said. "She had been seen several times standing on the street where the cemetery used to be, her head bowed in prayer, wearing what appears to be a wedding dress. Until recently, we had no idea who she may have been."

But a possible answer came from an unlikely source. A letter found by Dr. Henry from a man named Hiram Berry, dated September 1822, spoke of a woman who gave birth to a son, only to die herself of complications a few days later. "A nice looking woman who lives on the same march as me." Hiram went on to say that she was "buried in her wedding dress; cream, trimmed in white lace, the only nice dress she owned. She looked beautiful with her head turned to one side and a smile on her face."

Today it's an empty building, most recently called the Canoe, a restaurant located at 515 S. Main Street. Known as Eckert's Tavern from 1818 to 1846, it is possibly the oldest bar west of the Mississippi River. In the summer of 2007, while Canoe's was open, there were rumors of people being touched on the leg by unseen hands, even hugs as if from a child on the legs of the adults there. These same kind of stories are heard from patrons of other businesses that have operated within this building.

Next door to Canoe's is a patio area. At one time, a building occupied the space until it burned. A small girl died in the fire—a child who actually had lived at 523 S. Main Street. Did the child start the fire? Or was she dead before the fire started? Unfortunately, the actual story will probably never be known, but the child refuses to allow people to forget her.

Another set of apparitions, which Michael calls generic ghosts for St. Charles, is known simply as the French couple. They have been reported at the Lewis and Clark restaurant, and strolling down the street farther south. A couple, possibly the same couple, has been heard arguing in French inside the Little Hills Winery and Restaurant. The man has a handlebar mustache and wears a brown houndstooth jacket; the beautiful woman wears a bright red dress. Next door to the Lewis and Clark is a small park which, according to Michael, was once a small, elite cemetery, founded by Dr. Jeremiah Millington, which was also later moved.

The Little Hills Winery, at 501 S. Main, was built around 1860. Employees have reported lightweight items being knocked around with a lot more noise than a dropped napkin would be expected to make. Along with the French couple arguing, this keeps the employees on edge. Michael believes this was the location where a French man beat his wife to death in the misty past. Local legend says they were buried in Millington's cemetery, which is now in the courtyard next to the Lewis and Clark.

We discussed the Roy Cox building, where the original courthouse once stood with the gallows in the rear. Here I photographed orbs in three consecutive photos, as if it were moving across the field by the building. According to Dr. Henry, the gallows were taken down in the early 20th century. We discussed some of the executions, including those of the Black brothers. Michael said his research suggested that the Black brothers were railroaded to the gallows. They had been major troublemakers in the past, and this was a good excuse to get rid of them. While there was no evidence of this in the papers or reports I found, of interesting note was the fact that, according to Michael, the sheriff who presided over their execution committed suicide a few months later in the apartments over the present-day Goellner Printing Company.

One of the buildings reportedly holds the spirit of a little girl who can be heard playing in the attic. The staff has named her "Emily". The I.O.O.F. building, one of the first skyscrapers, housed a bank on the main level, a vaudeville theater on the second level, and the local hall for the International Organization of Odd Fellows on the third floor. It was reported that at least four actors committed suicide inside the old theater. Former employees have reported doors opening and strange noises.

At the other end of the cobblestone street, two ghost dogs have been seen multiple times wandering down the center of Main Street, appearing legless. It is known that Lewis and Clark maintained some Newfoundland hounds on their exploration of the American West. During a recent tour, the new owners of one of the buildings overheard Michael's lecture and asked if he was going to talk about their ghost dogs, which they hear almost nightly playing and growling unseen outside the building.

One local business owner it seems broke the heart of one of the invisible inhabitants. Diane Rolen, co-owner of the popular metaphysical and inspirational bookstore, The Enchanted Attic, which is located at 308 South Main Street, recently moved from an upstairs space to a street level storefront. While the business was located above the cobblestone street, several small incidents occurred including a jar candle taking off its own lid!

Diane said at the end of business one day, she checked the scented jar candles because guests like to open them and check the aroma, not always replacing the jar lids tightly. She checked all the jars, then started to walk away. As she turned her back, she heard a "bing" sound, and the Mason-type jar lid popped off the top of the jar she had just checked, and flipped end over end to the floor below. This was typical of the tricks played there.

But after moving to the lower shop, the upstairs spirit had a new tactic. Diane sent an employee upstairs to pick up a box left there earlier. She expected the young girl to be awhile but the employee came down immediately with a story to tell.

The young girl said she heard loud sobbing filling the room upstairs. She told the ghost it could come down and visit anytime as the new shop was in the same building. The sobbing continued until the girl left.

Historic Downtown St. Charles is possibly one of the most haunted cities in Missouri. Tours fill up quickly around Halloween so Michael gives the tour throughout the year. Bring along a camera and you may pick up some spirits of your own.

After all, to the well-organized mind, death is but the next great adventure.

—Dumbledore

Harry Potter & The Sorcerer's Stone by J. K. Rowling

Photo by Dan Terry

The Garth Woodside Mansion *was a favorite stopover for author Samuel Clemens. The owners say the building, now a bed & breakfast, is definitely haunted.*

Marion County, Missouri

Chapter 13

Hannibal Ghosts

this Mississippi River town hosts the ghosts

In 1680, the French monk, Louis Hennepin, came up the Illinois River to the Mississippi, continuing his river trek. He saw a large creek, which had cut a gorge a quarter of a mile across, spilling its contents into the Mississippi. A family of brown bears drank, fished and played on its banks near the convergence of the two waterways. Hennepin called the area Bear Creek.

It would be a century before another explorer spent any time in this area. Hennepin renamed the stream Hannibal Creek after the ancient general. More and more people eventually moved to the area, fighting the elements, floods and Indians to build a village along the banks of the slow, peaceful Mississippi. In 1818, Marion County was platted and named after the famous Revolutionary War hero Francis "The Swamp Fox" Marion.

Hannibal was laid out in 1836 and chartered in 1845 with some 2000 people. During the Civil war, the people of Hannibal leaned quietly toward the Southern way, while Union troops occupied the area, keeping the important river port city for Northern interests. During the time of Mark Twain, the city boasted two newspapers, including one started by Orion Clemens where his brother, Samuel Clemens, or Mark Twain, learned the newspaper business and discovered he had a knack for writing.

Hannibal had two hardware stores, 14 dry goods stores, two sawmills for the large lumber demand and four slaughterhouses that sent pork and beef to St. Louis and beyond.

Hannibal was also well within the communication loop. Stagecoaches stopped three times a week, bringing the mail. Steamboats came into port daily, reporting on news. A ferry carried passengers and information across the river to the Illinois side. Hannibal's history includes the railroad, which came through in 1859. In 1860, the General Grant, a 34-ton steam engine, was the first steam train engine built on the west side of the Mississippi. Two years later, the first railroad mail car to be built in the United States was built at Hannibal.

Of course, Mark Twain is not the only Hannibal resident to become world famous and beloved. In 1867, Margaret "Maggie" Toben was born in a small shack at Hannibal which stands today as a museum. Maggie yearned for more than marriage to a poor Irish laborer. She followed her brothers to Colorado, with the intention of marrying into money. Maggie wanted only to provide for her aging father the things he could never afford. However, she met J. J. Brown, a poor, self-educated man, and she fell in love. After much soul searching, she decided that happiness was better than money, and married him, despite his poverty. She earned fame after she was personally involved in a news story that captured worldwide attention. The result was a Broadway play that not only changed her name, but brought her international attention.

The incident was the sinking of the Titanic, and the play was "The Unsinkable Molly Brown." Maggie was aboard that doomed liner on the cold April night in 1912 when history was made but her reputation for being a tough, strong-willed Missouri woman started before that. Maggie fought for women's rights and assisted in soup kitchens in Colorado, feeding the poor families of the miners. She argued for a change in the juvenile justice system, and ran for Congress in 1909 and 1914, nearly unheard of for women.

Her primary claim to fame was the Titanic disaster, where she rallied the other women in her lifeboat to force the coxswain to return for more injured and drowning people at risk to her own life.

Safely aboard the Carpathia, a nearby ship that assisted in the rescue of the survivors, she continued to bring comfort and assistance to the injured and dying. When asked by a journalist about her amazing survival, she called the whole incident "Typical Brown luck," adding, "We're unsinkable!"

Hannibal has its share of famous residents. Most have moved on.

Some of them, however, cling to their hometown even after death.

Hannibal has many haunted places to call its own, from the Mark Twain Cave, made famous in Twain's novel "Tom Sawyer", to the Rockcliff Mansion. Twain even wrote about a local haunted house in his novels of Americana. But most haunted homes are not as famous.

Located at 301 N. Fifth Street, the Garden House Bed and Breakfast sits on a quiet street within easy walking distance of the old fashioned downtown district of Hannibal. A pretty blue-and-white building sitting on the corner and surrounded by plants, it was built in 1896 by Albert Wells Pettibone Jr., son of the founder of Hannibal Saw Mill and Sash Companies, and one of the leading philanthropists in the state. Being the heir apparent to a lumber baron's fortune, professional woodworkers were hired to fill the house with oak and mahogany woodwork, featured in the parlors, fireplace mantels and bedrooms.

The house is located on what was once known as Millionaires' Row and, accordingly, kept up the reputation of the neighborhood.

Albert and his wife were blessed with one child, William, who was born in the house. Tragically, Albert did not live to see the child grow up. Albert Pettibone died in his house at the age of 29 when his son was only one year old. The house was sold to Charles Trowbridge, owner of the Duffy-Trowbridge Stove Manufacturing Company. In 1905, this company was voted Hannibal's most important home industry. Duffy-Trowbridge was the sole provider of stoves and fireplace inserts to Montgomery Ward, whose catalogs were distributed to homes and outhouses nationwide. It was later sold to a furniture storeowner.

In 2003, Chris Bobek came into town visiting friends who had moved to Hannibal during an era when the city was attempting to attract artists to the area. Chris immediately fell in love with the building, which was badly in need of restoration. Chris took on this labor of love, first as a home away from home, then as a bed and breakfast owner. The old residents, unseen at the time, soon let their presence be known.

"During renovation," Chris told me, "we could hear music from the attic—violin music, actually. More than once, we followed it to the attic door, and could hear it from outside. But, as soon as we opened the door, the music would stop. And we never found where it was coming from."

But the spirit did not only play music, but was ready to work as well. Chris related, "People heard a sound coming from the basement such as would be made by sawing with a hand saw. They'd ask, but I seldom use a handsaw! So we'd track it to the basement, and we could hear it too, but as soon as we opened the door, it would stop."

Overnight guests have also had experiences there. Two women stayed together in the East Room upstairs. Chris said the first day, they were outgoing and friendly. On the second morning of their stay, both were unusually quiet.

"They finally told me what happened. One of them awoke with the feeling that they were being stared at. She looked up, and saw a black shadow standing at the foot of the bed, appearing to be just watching them. She quietly nudged her friend, who also saw the black apparition standing and watching. The two women pulled the blanket up over their heads, and said they were so scared they could not even scream!"

A few moments later they peeked out and the shadow man was gone. They spent the rest of the night on silent vigil, unable to sleep.

Another couple spent the night there, but not alone in the bed. As the woman attempted to cuddle up to her husband, the man seemed to move away from her. She asked why he was pushing her away.

But her husband thought she was cuddled up next to him. When they both looked, there was a shadow lying between them. It disappeared almost as soon as it was seen and they could once again sleep closely. Which they did—out of fear.

In 2006, the Today Show sent a team of paranormal investigators to the Garden House for a Halloween special. What they discovered was an energy on the east corner of the living room, the east bedroom and the east corner of the attic, as if the energy radiated down the side of the building. As they walked through, the camera continued to turn itself off in the east section of each floor.

The team went into the attic and, at the east corner, the investigator's assistant fainted. The investigator himself, with some 30 years of experience in ghost hunting, turned white and had to leave the attic!

"We got downstairs," Chris related, "and the man asked me what to do! I said, 'You're the expert!'"

The investigator told Chris that, in 30 years, he had never felt a presence that strong. At first, he thought it was a negative energy. But he pulled himself together, went back upstairs, and attempted to make contact with the entity. This time, the investigator told Chris, he had made contact and discovered that the spirit is the ghost of the builder, Albert Pettibone Jr. He is young, well educated, and not a negative force. The spirit just wanted to let people know he was there. It was his wish to continue his existence in the home he loved.

But Pettibone is not the only resident to die at a young age, nor is he the only spirit to remain. According to Chris, Trowbridge also had a son who died at the age of three. While his mortal life is over, his spirit is believed to be playing in the halls of his former home.

Chris said that the upstairs hallway has a sensor so that lights come on when people are walking around at night. According to Chris and the guests, the lights come on and off by themselves as if unseen persons were walking the halls. They can hear footsteps and notice that the lights come on sporadically, not in a row as if someone was walking down the hall, but more at random.

One day, Chris heard a noise coming from the kitchen that he described as the sound of concrete being scraped. He later discovered the grate had been removed, apparently dragged across the ceramic tile to the center of the floor.

As recently as early April 2008, guests told him the next morning of hearing the sound of violin music coming from the attic—a ghostly serenade for the visiting couple.

Arif Dagin, a Turkish student attending college in the Hannibal area, works for Chris taking care of the guests. Arif did not believe in ghosts. He does now.

It started with little things, just letting Arif know the ghosts were around. "I fixed the table at night for breakfast," Arif said. "the first morning, the silverware for the place at the head of the table, had been moved and was spread around the table. No other place setting had been touched."

Arif believed the guests had done it, and fixed it. The next morning, it happened again. "Just the one place setting was disturbed, and moved all over the table." It happened a third time, the following day. This time, there had been no guests in the house. At least, not any living guests. "I kept saying I don't believe, I don't believe," Arif told me. "Now it's okay, I believe."

But the spirits were not done playing with Arif. One cold, snowy night the city of Hannibal was completely snowed in. The roads were closed, and Chris was in Chicago. There were no guests and Arif had the house to himself.

"I made sure the screen door was locked from the inside, and the heavy front door was locked." Arif related. "I went to bed around 10 P.M., and later awoke to the sound of stomping down in the main floor."

Believing that someone had broken in, he attempted to call the police. However, he had left the phone in a charger downstairs. Picking up a wine bottle for protection, Arif searched the house. The front door was still locked, and he began searching the upstairs rooms.

"I could hear running. I went upstairs, and there was nothing. I searched each room, under the beds and in the closets. I returned to the hall and as I walked down the hall, I could hear footsteps, like it was following me. I couldn't see it, but it would stop after I stopped and start again when I walked. Okay, I believe!"

Arif called Chris, who confirmed he was still in Chicago. When Arif told the story, Chris said it must be the ghost.

Arif also has a photograph he took of the dining room, reported to be one of the most haunted rooms of the house. Others have reported photos of strange apparitions, as well as "people" in the photo who were not present when it was taken. One guest photographed the painted flowers on the wall of the dining room, only to find, on one photo only, that the painted greenery was gone, replaced by a white wall similar to the original when Chris bought the place.

Arif's photo, which he has made into postcards and gives to anyone interested, was one of several taken. This, according to Arif, is the only one that has a mist across it. There is also what appears to be the face of a small boy in the middle of the table—as if he raised his head up through the table top for a picture. Of more interest was one of the chairs, in which no one was sitting at the time. The photo shows the distinct shadow of a head as if someone is sitting at the table, watching the child.

A night at the Garden House Bed and Breakfast may be the paranormal adventure you're craving. The spirits seem friendly, as are your hosts. Even down to the afternoon cookies, turning down the feather beds, and the ghostly violin serenade in the night.

The Garden House is not the only bed and breakfast in Hannibal with its own shadow guests. The Garth Woodside Mansion, located just outside the city limits of Hannibal, offer rooms with fireplaces, fresh warm cookies, whirlpool baths, and somewhat quieter spirits.

Samuel Clemens, also known by the pen name, Mark Twain,

was born November 30, 1835, in Florida, Missouri. At the age of four, he moved with his family to the quaint Mississippi River town of Hannibal, which became the model for the fictional town of St. Petersburg in the Tom Sawyer and Huckleberry Finn novels.

After Clemens worked a stint for his brother Orion Clemens on the newspaper, he became a steamboat pilot. He found a position for another brother, Henry, as a mud clerk on the *Pennsylvania.* Henry Clemens was killed in an explosion on that riverboat, and Mark Twain blamed himself for the rest of his life for causing his brother's death. He had dreamed of the death of his brother on the ship more than a month before it happened. That dream spurred an interest in the paranormal, and Clemens became an early member of the Society for Psychical Research.

During the Civil War, Clemens attempted to form a militia unit for the Confederacy. That group fell apart after two weeks and Clemens moved West.

After a long career of writing and befriending Presidents and European royalty, as well as winning the hearts and minds of people all over the world, Clemens had another premonition, this time of his own death. In 1909, Clemens said "I came in with Halley's Comet in 1835. It's coming again next year, and I expect to go out with it. . . . The Almighty has said, no doubt, "Now here are two unaccountable freaks. They came in together, they must go out together."

Clemens died the next day after the comet returned, on April 21, 1910. But did he leave the earthly plane?

Clemens returned to Hannibal several times to visit his childhood friends, John and Helen Garth. John's dad owned a cigar factory, which Clemens spoke of with fond memories. After school, John attended the University of Missouri in Columbia, then returned to Hannibal to help his brother with the cigar factory. During the Civil War, Garth and his family went to New York City, where he engaged in banking, brokerage and manufacturing.

John Garth returned to Hannibal in 1871, where he formed a bank and took up ranching. He built a summer home which he called Woodside, a large mansion located some three miles from Hannibal. It was here that Clemens enjoyed his many stays with the people he had based some of his characters on.

Garth passed away in 1899, but Clemens continued to be a guest

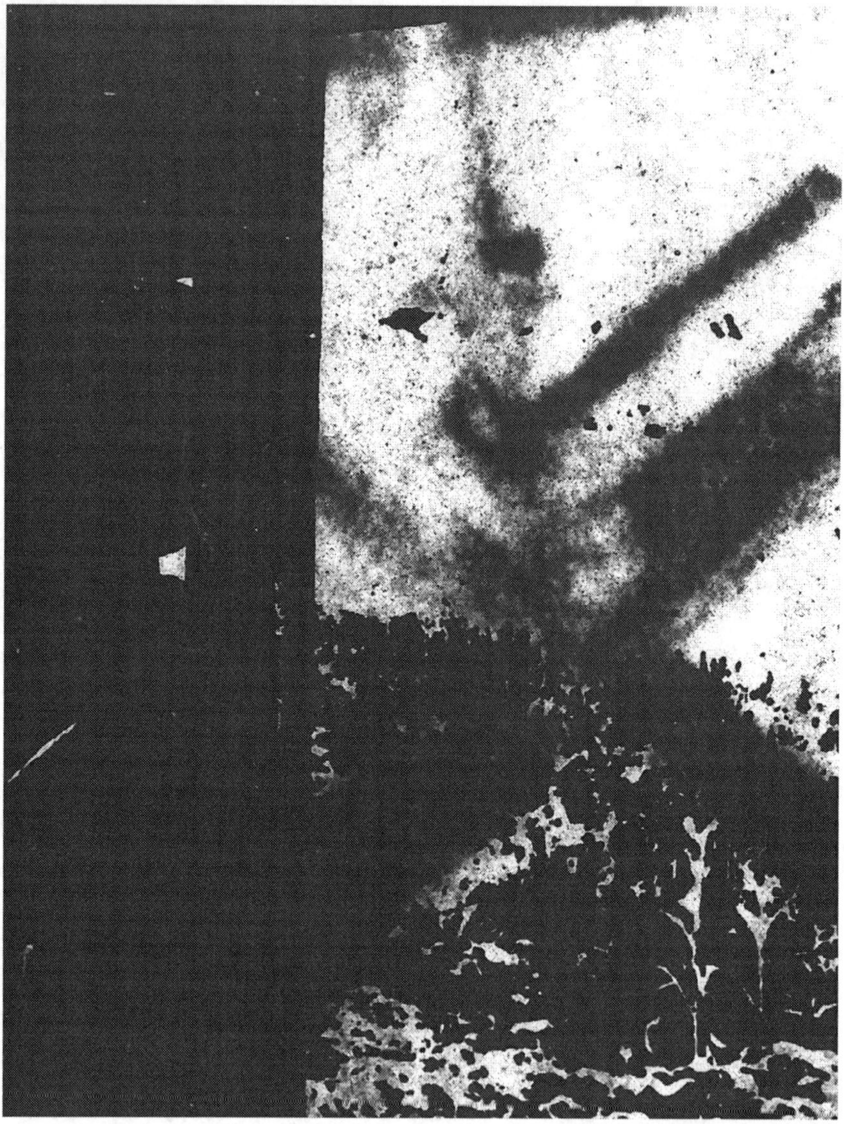

Photo by Lorra Gleitz

***This figure appeared outside the Garth Bed and Breakfast** at Hannibal, out toward the woodshed. Note that it resembles a man with an ax in his head.*

of his widow and her daughter.

In the 1990's, John and Julie Rosen purchased the mansion, becoming the sixth owners since it was built in 1871. Today, it is one of the finest B and B's in the state, along with the Dowager Cottage on the grounds.

An employee at a local convenience store told me the Garth Mansion is haunted. Lorra Gleitz, an amateur photographer, had taken photos of her family while there a year earlier. When she inverted the photos, one had what appeared to be the shadow of a gravestone on the old ice house. Another, once inverted, which changes it to black and white, clearly showed a male face and what appears to be an ax almost in his head. Lorra provided me with the photos. I searched my usual sources, finding nothing about the Garth Woodside Mansion being haunted. However, she was determined and since I was in the area, I stopped off and asked.

I spoke with John, who said he didn't really believe in ghosts at the Garth. Sure, he had seen some interesting photos taken by others, including what appeared to be faces in the old ice house. But, who would want to be there?

He suggested I speak with his wife, who was working at the family store in downtown Hannibal. When I arrived there, Julie had more to talk about.

"A lot of the guests get orb photos," Julie told me. "And one of the families that lived here had a young son who died in Kansas City. Several people say they've felt something, and have reported hearing a child's voice."

Perhaps more interesting is in the Samuel Clemens room. "This is the room where Mark Twain stayed, and several people have reported the smell of cigar smoke there, even though no one has smoked in the house for years."

The Woodside Mansion is a beautiful old museum-quality establishment surrounded by 130-year-old oaks and by the natural setting that characterizes rural Missouri. And an added bonus would be a frank discussion with one of the wisest men in American history, Samuel Clemens. But ask him not to smoke in the rooms.

Photo by Dan Terry

***The Gasconade River** was the scene of a grisly train wreck in 1855 in which 31 people died and 70 more were injured.*

Gasconade County, Missouri

Chapter 14

River Disaster

no rest for the innocent

The train continued through the cold, rainy day. Between the cities of Hermann and Gasconade, the train passed the steamer Ben Holt, which was carrying passengers down river. Boat and train travelers waved and shouted greetings to each other. It was 1:00 P.M. and the rain was not letting up but the spirits of the 600 people could not be dampened.

It was November 1, 1855. The Missouri-Pacific Railroad had completed its track from St. Louis to Jefferson City. The company was throwing a party, inviting dignitaries from St. Louis for the official opening of the railway. The owners of the railroad company were hoping to impress these people, looking forward to help in getting more lucrative contracts. A large dinner and celebration awaited the ten carloads of prestigious guests, basically representing the Who's Who of St. Louis society. Some of the special guests on the train were former St. Louis County Clerk Henry Choteau, Rev. Dr. Bullard of the First Presbyterian Church, St. Louis Mayor Washington King, E.C. Blackburn, President of the Board of Alderman, Justice of the Peace Mann Butler, and State Legislators T.J. Mutt and E. B. Jefferies.

The train was approaching the 900-foot bridge crossing the Gasconade River. At first, the engineer wanted to stop and check out the bridge for safety. The day before, an engine and construction train had been taken back and forth across the bridge on a test run, but the weight of the party train was much greater than that of the construction train. In a scene reminiscent of the Titanic incident 57 years hence, a decision was made to place the safety of the passengers second to time. They were running late and had to catch up.

The train, along with the tender car supplying fuel and water, ten carloads of partygoers, and another engine began crossing the bridge over the swollen Gasconade River. As the engine reached the second pier, the bridge gave way. The engine went over, pulling several cars with it, falling 30 feet to the river below. The engine turned and landed, falling back on the timbers and cars, pining people under its weight. The St. Louis newspaper *The Daily Missouri Democrat* that day related the following:

The crash and the shriek of the passengers as the bridge gave way are represented as most terrible. The forward engine having just reached the second pier, went down with the train and, as it fell, turned completely over, and back upon the nearest cars, crushing the timber and passengers in the most appalling manner.

As reported in *The Daily Missouri Democrat* on Nov. 3, 1855:

At the time of the accident, a severe thunderstorm was prevailing and it is related to us that the merciless pouring of the rain and the roar and flash of the angry tempest mingling with the cries of the wounded and dying made up a picture harrowing beyond anything the mind can imagine.

Included among the revelers were two groups of military musicans. Along with the other less-injured passengers, they began immediately helping each other. Locals from the City of Gasconade opened their hearts and homes to the survivors. A building less than 100 yards from the bridge was used as a makeshift hospital and morgue.

Before the day was done, 31 people had died, and another 70 people were injured. Homes in nearby Hermann were also used to house survivors. Another train was dispatched from St. Louis to pick up the injured and dead, but on the way back to St. Louis, a second bridge gave way just past New Haven, bringing the rescue train to a halt. Locals helped build rough coffins as a steamer was sent to pick up the injured, further delaying their return to their homes.

While heroic stories of rescues and rescuers prevailed, not all were so honorable. As related in the weekend edition of *The Daily Missouri Democrat:*

> *A number of scoundrels, who gathered at the scene, were discovered soon afterwards attempting to rob the bodies of the dead. In some instances, they took off even the boots from the mutilated bodies.*

Reportedly, Henry Choteau, a member of one of the oldest and most influential families of St. Louis, was so disfigured that he was identified only by his invitation ticket. This tragedy would serve as Gasconade's biggest claim to fame.

Gasconade County was established in 1820. Isaac Best had built a grist mill in 1811 at the mouth of the Gasconade River, where the first county seat was later established. Reportedly, the final choice for a state capitol city was narrowed down to Gasconade or Jefferson City, with Jefferson City winning by only two votes.

In 1823, the town was called Gasconade Ferry because a licensed ferry crossed there. Losing the state capitol bid, Gasconade had to settle for being the county seat, but that was only until 1825. The county seat was moved downstream to Hermann due to the serious annual flooding at Gasconade.

Today, the city has little commerce to speak of, and less manufacturing. Because of its distance to Hermann and its location, Gasconade became known as a wild village with little law enforcement.

The building that was used as a temporary morgue was

eventually replaced with a larger building, built and used during the days of railroad travel. The two-story brick structure, like many others built near railroads, has seen better days. In the past, the building has been used as a hotel, and later as a brothel. It's served as a general store and as a tavern multiple times.

Today, the building still has the old bar, jukebox and decorations as when it was a bar. The current owner, identified as Drew, purchased the building in 1996 and keeps his Harley Davidson motorcycle parked inside the old bar section.

Drew and Donna have had multiple experiences in the building, in which Drew has lived for 15 years. Strange noises, doors began shutting themselves, quietly at first then slamming shut. Voices and shadow apparitions were seen and heard near a room where Drew states a man shot himself to death in the past.

The spirit seems to like things open. One guest, who contacted Missouri Paranormal Research about the incident, said the doorknob on the room she stayed in was shaking violently several times during the night for several minutes each time. Drew said that he cannot keep the antique door knob on the door as it works itself out or falls out the following day, no matter how hard he turns the screws.

Drew related a story to the first investigation team that a guest had been staying the night with a small child, approximately age six. The child stated she saw a man in that room with no head. The mother of the child told her to tell the man to "go to the light", to which the child replied "He said he ain't going nowhere."

According to local legend, a man was shot in the head outside the bar and a girl was raped there. Information on only one murder has been found.

The first stories of the incident were interesting. As reported in the Gasconade County newspaper, *The Advertiser-Courier,* on January 3, 1990, at approximately 1:30 A.M. on December 31, 1989, a gunfight took place in the streets of Gasconade. Ronald Redwine, 24, was killed. Larry Tune, 32 and Dennis Kobusch, 30 were wounded in the exchange. According to Sheriff Bob Mathis, early investigation showed that Redwine took a shotgun from Gary Tune, brother of Larry Tune. Redwine then shot Larry Tune, who returned fire with a rifle, striking Redwine in the head. Redwine managed to get one last shot off before succumbing to the fatal injury, striking Larry Tune again and also Kobusch, who was standing nearby.

At that time, more interviews were scheduled. Some 30 people were interviewed, and a completely different story emerged.

The January 17, 1990 headline in *The Advertiser-Courier* proclaimed, "Victim never fired a shot!"

According to the article, Larry and Gary Tune had caught a young man named John Blackburn, 19, slashing their tires. They had beaten the younger man, who had run away threatening to return later with friends for revenge.

Around midnight, a group of people approached the tavern. It is uncertain if Blackburn was with them or if the group was in any way involved with him. Gary Tune fired a shot into the air. It is also uncertain if he was shooting to warn the group away, or simply celebrating the New Year.

At that time, Ronald Redwine was passing the tavern. Believing the shooting may have endangered him, he dropped off his girlfriend and returned to confront Gary Tune. According to the article, Redwine had taken the shotgun away from Gary Tune, and began emptying the weapon onto the ground by pumping rounds out of the ejection port.

While he was unloading the weapon, probably looking down at the gun as he did so, he was shot in the head with a hunting rifle by Larry Tune, killing him instantly. Tests on the hands confirmed that Redwine had never fired a shot.

Seeing what happened, Gary Redwine, brother of the victim, drove by the spot and fired at least two rounds from a shotgun at the Tunes, striking Larry Tune and accidentally hitting Kobusch in the process. Larry Tune was charged with first degree murder and armed criminal action as a result of the shooting spree. Gary Redwine was charged with first degree assault and armed criminal action. And John Blackburn was charged with first degree tampering. Sheriff Robert Mathis stated, "I personally think that if Blackburn hadn't slashed the tires, there'd have been no altercation and Ronald would still be alive."

With such a history, there is no doubt the possibility of haunting exists. On April 14, 2007, MPR did the first investigation there. Involved was founder Steven LaChance and lead investigator

Greg Myers, along with psychic Theresa Reavy, Tim Clifton, and others. This investigation convinced the ghost hunters that the place was very haunted. The swinging doors leading into the bar opened by themselves when approached by the investigators. A human shadow was seen by two people moving quickly from a room. Voices were heard by the investigators, and one saw a grapefruit-sized orb on the second floor. A piece of plaster was thrown at investigators, even though no plaster existed in the building anymore!

A second investigation was planned but the MPR team was forced to divide into two teams to cover another investigation. At that time, Spookstalker was invited along.

I met Drew and Donna, and was given a tour of the house. Once again, I decided to stick with Tim and Theresa. We started upstairs where a shadow person was seen briefly.

Both Tim and Theresa, psychics with MPR, sensed an angry male in the room of the unconfirmed suicide. They also believed the spirit of a little girl being held prisoner by the angry spirit was in the room. Drew and Donna left the building, allowing us free access. We then went into the small apartment they used, and photographed a few orbs and heard footsteps in the hallway outside the room. Tim quickly opened the door, finding an empty hall and stairway.

We changed places with the team members downstairs, and worked inside the bar. Shadows and noises were quickly explained by traffic outside. Theresa believed there was a spirit in the back corner. I went to the corner in an attempt to flush it out. Photographs showed a large number of orbs around me where none had been photographed earlier.

Finally, after a rest outside, we went into the area where the bodies of the dead and dying reportedly were taken after the accident. In this room, psychics on the last investigation had stated there were several spirits, including one male walking around with a hole in his stomach and a female spirit killed in the accident. They also felt a intense spirit, which repeated the word, "Why?" They believed it was Redwine, upset because his body had laid in the street for so long. Not realizing he was dead, he wanted to know why no one helped him.

At that time, we did not have the true story of the shooting. Investigators had been told that the shooting had occurred inside the bar and that he had been shot trying to protect his brother. This was the story I based the EVP session on.

It was approximately 11:00 P.M. There was enough light from the streetlights outside that we could see the back of the room through the archway. Investigators had placed a video camera in the next room, and we could see the light on the camera. Tim began speaking to the spirit, receiving no answer.

After 20 minutes, Tim invited me to speak to the ghost. I began speaking to the spirit, and the odor of cigarettes filled the room. We could all see shadows moving in the next room, teasing us, not coming close enough for a good sighting. We heard noises in the next room. Low voices. Things being moved.

Tim mentioned the Tri-County Truck Stop, and the similarities here. As we began talking about the incident, the noise and shadow movement in the next room increased. Suddenly, the sound of papers being shoved off a table and fluttering to the floor was heard. Once before, on an investigation in Berger, I began ignoring the ghost when he would not make himself known. It suddenly became more active, as if ignoring the ghost, like ignoring a child, would bring it out.

This seem to confirm that theory. I told Tim, "Someone's being ignored." Suddenly, Sherri mentioned that she could no longer see the light on the camera. Indeed, we could see the archway but a black mass, churning on itself like a cartoon storm, was blocking view into the next room.

I then stood up and demanded the spirit leave. Tim, who can hear the spirits, said the spirit was saying no. I spoke to the spirit like I would during a police interview, pushing it, making it angry. "Yes, you've been killed. You were shot in the head. It's a very unpleasant way to die but you can take solace in the fact that you saved your brother's life. You don't belong here anymore."

Tim abruptly said, "NO!" Lowering his voice, Tim said "Dan, it's saying you're wrong. Over and over again." I continued pushing the ghost to leave, go to the next world. Tim continued to say, "No, No."

Suddenly, during this disagreement between the ghost and me, I saw Sherri, who was sitting next to Tim across the room from me, jump to her feet and slam her hand across her mouth. Her arms were tight across her body. At nearly the exact moment, Tim exclaimed,

"Something just brushed past me!"

At the time when Sherri jumped, Tim said he felt a cold rush of air go past him, brushing his arm. Once Sherri could speak, she said she felt a cold rush go through her. Sherri described the feeling of gooseflesh all over her body, including the bottoms of her feet. She said while taking in a breath, she could not get air or breathe out for three seconds. She also described it as an electrical current running through her body.

Tim said the ghost had gone through them to reenact its own death. The room seemed to brighten somewhat, with the spirit leaving. We could now see the light on the camera again. Tim and Theresa both believed the ghost was gone, and we went outside for a break.

After shutting down the investigation, Tim and Theresa went back upstairs alone to pray for the spirit of the child, attempting to release it. When he returned, Tim said he had angered the male spirit to the point that it choked him as he prayed for the child. Theresa believed the spirit of the girl managed to leave during that time.

We left the City of Gasconade with little hard evidence. No good photos or EVP's this round. But, throughout the years of investigation, Sherri complained she had never been touched, grabbed, or shoved as the rest of us had been. Tonight, she got her wish, as the spirit flooded her for a moment. She's just a little more of a believer than before.

To be alone in this place would not be so bad during the day, although a certain chill seems to be in the atmospere even at the sunniest noontime. But, no one could want to be left there after dark.

—Susy Smith,
Author, *Prominent American Ghosts*

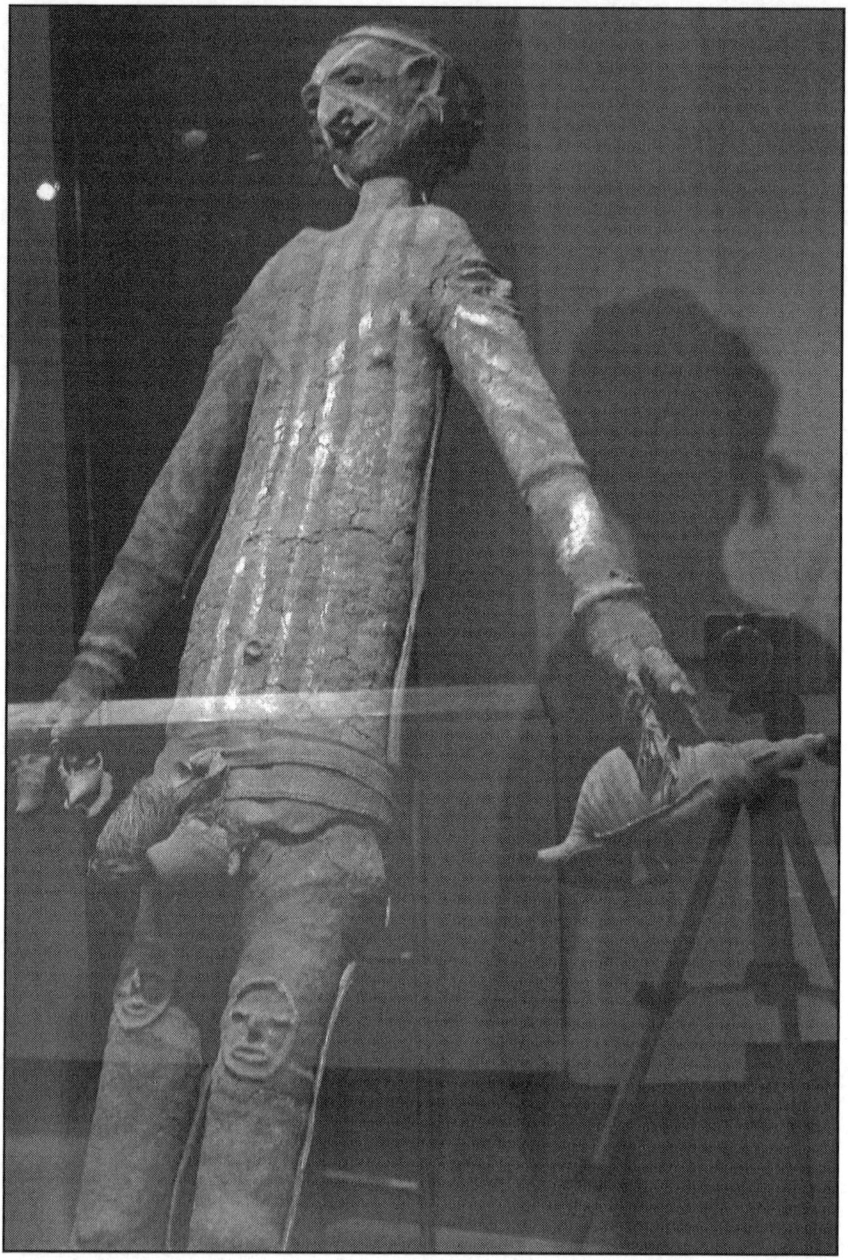

Photo by Dan Terry

***This life-sized effigy from the Pacific island of Vanuatu** is made of wood, bamboo, and other materials, and is topped with the actual skull of a deceased native. Called rambaramp, this one is on display at the St. Louis Art Museum and he wants out of the glass display case!*

St. Louis City, Missouri

Chapter 15

It is Alive!

like the movie mummies, something stalks the halls of the St. Louis Art Museum

Jimmy Buffett sings of life in the tropical zone. Peaceful, easy, warm days on the beach, hammocks between two palm trees as beautiful native girls serve cold, tropical rum drinks.

However, the series of Pacific islands known as the nation of Vanuatu has a dark history that has little to do with the island paradise of Jimmy's songs. Cannibalism, attacking ships and crews, and even blackbirding, or long-term indentured servitude, similar to slavery, existed on these islands. Along with these unholy activities, the natives practiced the magical art of rambaramp.

Not long after the death of a high-ranking man of the village, an effigy was made of his body. His real body was taken out to the jungle and drained. The life-size effigy was made from wood, bamboo, and other vegetable matter. The head was removed from the decomposing corpse, and the skull was over modeled with resin and fiber by a master rambaramp-maker to resemble the dead man. The body of the effigy was painted and decorated in accordance with the rank and social standing of the deceased at the time of his passing.

The skull of the deceased was believed to hold the spirit; the body was built and decorated to give dignity to that spirit. All of this was used for spirit communication as well as ancestor worship.

When the effigy was finished, complete with the reconstructed head and face made over the skull, a large feast was held with many pigs, which the locals believed were magical creatures, being killed. After this, the new body for the spirit was placed in the Men's House, for the spirit to finish entering the body. From that point on, every few years another celebration was held to give strength to the spirit. After 20 years, the spirit was free to depart and the effigy lost its strength forever. One last celebration, and the ritual was done.

But did the spirit always leave the effigy? And if the spirit body was moved, would the spirit follow? Even half-way around the world?

Inside the St. Louis Art Museum, located in Forest Park, a rambaramp sits at an odd angle inside a glass display case. Originally from the South Malakula Island, Melanesia, it is believed to be a 20th century effigy, complete with the human skull covered and recreated to look like the deceased. The guide on the tour explained why the body was at an angle to all the other displays. It's unhappy.

The rambaramp was donated to the museum by Morton D. May, heir to the Famous-Barr department store chain. His grandfather, David May, started a store called "Famous" in St. Louis, later purchasing the William Barr Dry Goods store and creating Famous-Barr. Morton May led a privileged life, attending private St. Louis schools and going on to Dartmouth. In spite of his wealthy upbringing and influential family, he began his career working summers in the complaint department. He later held every job in the business, from stock boy to president of the company, and finally chairman of the board.

In the early 1940's, prior to World War II, Morton began collecting artwork. Cubists, American, and German expressionist to start, but soon he began collecting indigenous arts of primitive cultures, including African and Oceanic tribes such as those of the Vanuatu Island.

Morton May donated some 3000 art objects to the St. Louis Art Museum, as well as loaning many pieces to that establishment and to the Washington University Gallery.

These pieces were bequeathed to the museums upon his death. Among his gifts were several figures from Oceanic tribes in the Pacific, including this rambaramp.

According to the guide, several times the museum had been opened and the early crew had discovered the glass case was broken from the inside out. The glass was replaced repeatedly, only to find it broken again later.

Eventually, someone checked with the experts. It was suggested that the spirit within the rambaramp had been taken from its native soil before the 20-year period was up. According to the information card within the glass case, it is believed to be a twentieth century piece.

The tour guide said it was suggested by the expert that the effigy be faced in another direction, and placed at an angle to slow its ability to gain strength from the earth. This was done, and the shattered glass ceased.

However, scratch marks have since been found on the inside of the glass. Today, the scratches can still be seen on the glass. Run a thumbnail across it; smooth on the outside, indicating the scratches are on the inside. There is a note at the bottom of the information plaque, saying:

> *There are some who think that this Ramparamp figure contains a spirit that lingers, and people have pointed out scratches on the glass pane in front of you as proof. As far as we can tell, the figure is not alive; the scratches were made by something harder than a dead*

man's fingernails.

"As far as we can tell, the figure is not alive." But, what if it is undead? What tests determine if the dead walks, unchecked by the living? If the curators do not believe the figure is alive, why did they take the precaution of tilting it?

Finally, perhaps the spirit is stronger than mortal fingernails. Notice the plaque does not say what scratched the glass, only their belief that it was not the nails of the dead.

This area of the museum, similar to the Egyptian section, is a place of the dead. In this space, are carved figures used for spirit communication and representations of the owner's death taken from burial caves, Tatanna masks used in association with sacred Malagan rites held in graveyards after death, and Yipwon, wooden figures used by sacred men to call upon their ancestors for help in hunting animals or revenge killings. To entice a spirit to enter a figure, it was smeared with animal feces, human meat and blood from a penis.

See the internal scratches, look into the blank eyes of the death mask over the human skull, and decide for yourself if this unholy creature may walk the halls of the museum in this exhibit of the dead.

Something is always happening, but when it happens, people don't always see it, or understand it, or accept it.

—John Hobbs
Fallen, 1998

Left: *General William Selby Harney.*

Below: **The Harney Mansion** *of Sullivan, Missouri, built in 1856. General Harney bought the mansion in 1872 after his retirement.*

Crawford County, Missouri

Chapter 16

An Officer and a Gentleman

an evening of hospitality with General Harney

The Harney mansion is haunted.

I was a student, transferred to Sullivan Elementary School from the tiny two-room schoolhouse in Stanton. The kids told me about the Harney Mansion. Rumors of ghosts, secret tunnels, Klan meetings and human sacrifices were created from the lurid minds of pre-adolescent boys, inflaming the imaginations of the new students.

As I got older, and was stimulated by the adventures of Carl Kolchack in "The Night Stalker", I couldn't wait to get inside the crumbling mansion and find the evil spirits dwelling within.

But, at the time, the crumbling structure was the stomping ground of older teens, drinking and using illegal drugs. I had seen the mansion in the light of day many times but never went inside and was never there at night. It was an imposing, frightening structure even in broad daylight.

Time goes by and now I'm over 40 and have been ghost hunting for years. Still, I had not been inside the mansion until after I received a phone call from Tim Clifton of MPR.

"Dan," Tim said, "I am giving you your dream. You are invited to assist MPR with an investigation in your old hometown, on July 21, at the Harney Mansion!"

In 1856, Dr. Alanson Leffingwell built the impressive mansion from native stone. He held onto it until 1872, when he sold it to retired Union General William Selby Harney.

Harney was born in Tennessee on August 27, 1800. His father, Major Thomas Harney, was a soldier in the Revolutionary War. Just up the road lived General Andrew Jackson, whose friendship would help the military career of the future general and Indian fighter.

With a war hero father, future president for a neighbor, and a brother who was an army surgeon, young William's career got off to a promising start. On his 18th birthday, William Selby Harney received a lieutenant's commission signed by President James Monroe.

Harney's military career began with Andy Jackson in Florida, where he helped run pirate Jean Lafitte off of United States soil and all the way back to Spain. Harney negotiated peace with Indians in Iowa, after which he was promoted to Captain. He served with some of the most famous people in American history, including Jefferson Davis, who was to become President of the Confederacy; and Abe Lincoln, who became President of the Union.

Soon Harney's reputation began to outshine his achievements. On June 27, 1834, he was charged in the state court at St. Louis, for the beating death of his slave, a female known as Hannah. No sentence was recorded, and popular belief is that the Army transferred him to avoid the negative publicity.

When the Chief of the Caloosa Indians went back on his agreement to maintain peace and attacked, Lt. Col. Harney not only hunted him down in his small village, but had him shot in the back as he attempted to escape. The body was retrieved, scalped, and hung with two other warriors in front of the village. The scalp was sent to headquarters in St. Augustine. Then the women and children of the village were sent to a reservation in Arkansas. The arrogant Harney was quoted in saying that if Secretary of War Joel Poinsett, whom Harney blamed for going back on his word and causing the chief to start a war, had been in the swamp, Harney would have hanged him alongside the brave chief.

The next adventure would take him to Mexico, where the officer became a hero after assaulting and capturing Cerro Gordo. When he captured 30 Irish American fighters assisting the Mexicans, Harney had them executed by hanging, including one man who had had both legs amputated. The surviving rebels were forced to bury the dead. To add insult to injury, Harney moved into the palace of an Incan prince.

During the battle of Ash Hallow, under command of General Harney, 85 men, women and children were killed in what has been described as a massacre. At this time, General Harney was nicknamed 'Butcher of the Brules.' In Utah, when the Mormons forced out the governor and federal judges, Harney was ordered to quell the religion-based uprising. His plan was to capture and execute Brigham Young and the 12 apostles and to move into the Mormon temple to show contempt for the would-be rebels. Before putting this plan into action, he was sent to another Indian uprising in the Pacific Northwest.

While in Washington and Oregon, Harney's temper nearly started a third war with England. On an island split down the middle, a pig owned by an Irish businessman on the English side crossed over and ate the potatoes on an American farm. With a temperamental leader on each side, the Canadian Governor and General Harney, war was nearly inevitable. Soon, 500 American soldiers with artillery were facing off against seven British warships. A calmer British officer made the decision to back down, saying "I will not send two great nations to war over a pig."

As the commanding officer of the Army Department of the West stationed in Missouri, General Harney was called to Washington D.C. for a conference. While his train was stopped in Harpers Ferry, Virginia, a young Confederate officer approached the General. When the lieutenant, apologizing for the inconvenience, informed Harney that he was now a prisoner of the Confederacy, General Harney replied with his usual kindly demeanor . . .

"God damn your soul!" The 61-year-old Union officer then began beating the young lieutenant. It took three officers to pull the older man off the young soldier, taking the General into custody.

Harney was sent to Richmond, Virginia, where he met with General Johnson and his old friend, Jefferson Davis. After refusing to join the Southern cause, Harney was returned to Washington D.C. and released.

William Selby Harney spent nearly 60 years in service to the United States. Some called him hero, some villain. Harney purchased the mansion from Leffingwell, adding a huge wing on the north side of the building, taking great care to use the same type of stone from the same

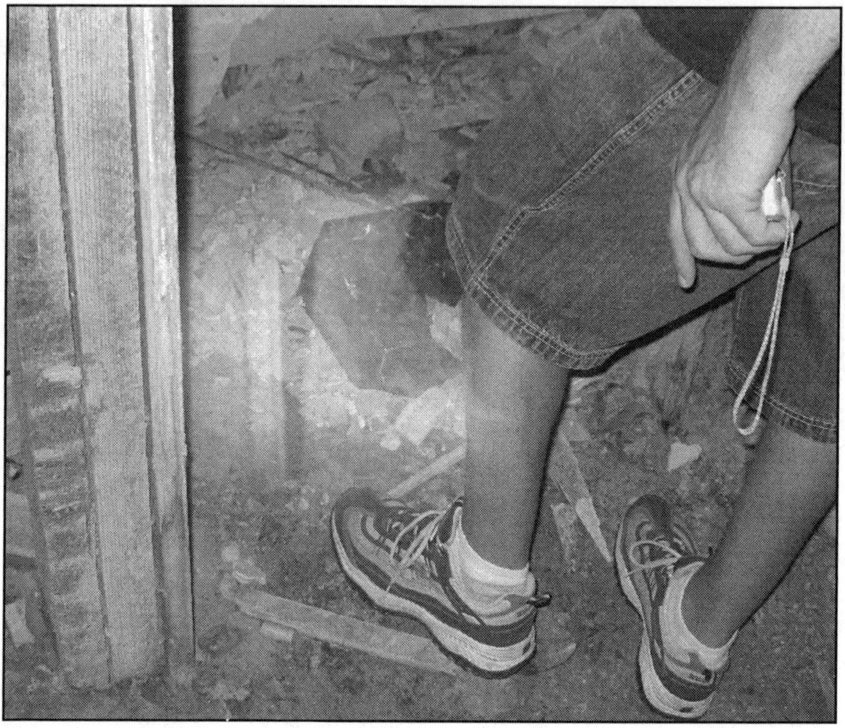

Photo by Tim Clifton

A mist surrounds an investigator's leg *in the Harney Mansion. Later, he felt something grab his leg.*

quarry to obtain the best match possible. The General used it as a summer home until 1874, when he moved to Florida. Harney died in Florida on May 9, 1889 and was buried in Arlington National Cemetery.

In 1896 Theodore Hinchcliff bought the thirty-plus room mansion. His wife, Lucy, was a singer with a remarkable contralto voice, a graduate of the prestigious Julliard school. Their daughter, Lucy Hinchcliff Riggan, became a concert pianist. The younger Lucy gave music lessons in the mansion and students reported she heated a cloth by the fireplace and placed it on the keys so they would be warm enough for her young students to practice. She married Sydney Riggan and lived in her own nearby home. Lucy Riggan kept the mansion until 1960, when the home was sold to Leo and Minerva Hollander.

For about 20 years, only a caretaker occupied the property, except on election days when it was utilized as a township polling place. When the mansion became totally unlivable, it served as a refuge for the homeless, including the drunks and narcotics users.

As time went by, what was once a huge mansion on hundreds of acres became a derelict building in a modest subdivision. Newer homes were built within yards of the old building. Inside, old fire pits, beer cans and needles littered the floor while birds flew among the rafters, oblivious to the misspelled curse words painted on the walls.

The property had fallen into serious disrepair by the time Paul and Geraldine Hollander Blesi deeded it over to the William S. Harney Historical Society. In 1984, the Harney Mansion was placed on the National Register of Historic Places. The Harney Foundation has worked hard to raise the funds to put a new roof on the building, warding off further deterioration, and plans to renovate the building when funds are made available.

MPR did an earlier investigation, making a video which revealed moving shadows and a mirror, which seemed to change the image inside with each shot, including an unidentified face. Investigators also observed an odor of cigars in one area, and the strong odor of lilacs in another.

When MPR returned, with Spookstalker in tow on that hot July night, we experienced several phenomena, some of which were cold spots, orbs, and strange EMF readings in the Leffingwell portion, where no electricity exists. Shadow people were seen moving both inside and outside the mansion by members of both my team and MPR. During an EVP session, Tim took a photo of me in a hallway, then noticed an orb behind me. When he told me, I immediately turned around and attempted to face my unseen audience. Tim took another photo, then announced that once again the spirit was behind me. We labeled this spirit, The Coward.

One room included an old dentist's chair that had been donated and placed there when plans called for the mansion to become a museum. In that room one investigator, who was being photographed by Tim Clifton, complained of being grabbed at the ankle. Later, the photographs showed what appeared to be a misty white hand with fingers grabbing the investigator's ankle.

During this time, another group was upstairs taking photos and doing their own EVP session. Investigators hung a weight from a string in one of the doorways and it began spinning in large circles quickly, although the string remained taunt. The weight became blurred with the speed of the circle. Theresa Reavey, psychic with MPR, began challenging the spirit. Suddenly, from the dark corner of the room, plaster was thrown at the investigators.

The two teams met downstairs in the parlor, a room that had been fixed up to represent the way it might have appeared in the years following the Civil War. At that time, we tried an EVP session to contact the General.

Being the only veteran in the room, I attempted an idea I had been nursing since being invited there. I pulled myself up in a semblance of attention, and addressed the General in a manner expected by a commanding officer.

When I asked for evidence of the General's presence, I and several others observed the curtain of a window move from the center inward, as if someone had moved it enough to peek inside. I continued, but Theresa Reavey said the spirit had left. Suddenly, the odor of cigar smoke filled the room and a black shadow, darker than the darkness, moved across the hallway.

Psychics believe there are three spirits in the mansion. One is an 18-year-old male who is very afraid of another spirit as well as of us. This is the one we call, "The Coward". A female spirit, who loves the parlor area, arrives with the odor of lilacs. And an angry, overbearing male spirit carries with him the odor of cigars.

On Saturday, October 6, 2007, I returned to the mansion. It was Harney Mansion Day, a celebration held in October each year which brings out people in period dress, including Civil War reenactors and others dressed as frontiersmen and town folks. Along with the peddlers and musical groups, the event brings in hundreds of people, all with human energy for the ghosts to feed off of. Steven LaChance brought a team from KLPW radio station, along with Theresa Reavey and Tim Clifton, to tape a ghost hunt for a Halloween special. They got more than they bargained for.

Sherri and I arrived early. Taking photos in the back of the mansion, looking directly at two trees, I saw a shadow person move quickly between the two trees, approximately 15 feet apart. I later discovered that a small cemetery once existed there, but the stones had long since been removed.

When Judy McPherson, working with the Harney Mansion Foundation arrived, Sherri and I went inside. While waiting for Tim and Steve to arrive, Sherri and I returned to the dentist room, where I challenged the ankle-grabbing spirit to try that on me. Sherri snapped photos of my legs while I made the challenge. A check of the photos showed a large black shadow coming from the floor and reaching up to my waist. The next photograph showed it receding back towards the floor, and the third was clear.

When Tim arrived, we both went back into the dentist's room, where once again I challenged the spirit while Sherri took photographs. This time, the first two photographs showed no problems. The third, taken from the same angle as the others at the same moment, showed a dark smear across the face of Tim Clifton. His face was completely covered by a black mass!

Diane Jones, radio personality with KLPW, arrived and instantly regretted being there.

The equipment was set up in preparation for the radio show. The program was to be taped, not live. Upstairs, the floor was not in good shape except down the center of the house. I set up warning lights along the walkway for the people going up there, and the soft glow was visible downstairs through the holes in the ceiling. While doing an EVP session, I was asked if the warning lights I had set up were blinking. I replied no, they were solid lights. Someone made the statement that they were blinking. We all looked up, and could see the lights fading off and on as if someone was blocking them while pacing along the walkway upstairs. A check later showed the batteries were good, and the blinking was not caused by the lights. What was up there?

During this session, a black mass, the same dark cloud seen last time, came down the hall, stopping just beyond the door. Psychic Theresa Reavey believed the other spirits, the coward and the lady, had left the room when this spirit walked in. When Tim asked if the spirits were being held against their will, we all could hear the word "yes" in a raspy voice coming from the next room. The sound could be heard on the tape and later on the broadcast show.

During the break, Tim and I, along with Sherri and Theresa, returned to the dentist room to stir things up a bit more. There, while doing an EVP session, I felt something grab my wrist, as if a doctor were gently checking my pulse. I could feel one finger on the veins, and several others on the wrist. I reached out and felt a cold spot, and Sherri and Theresa caught a phantom smell of rotting meat.

I began the next EVP session. I was coaxing down the ghost, and all could see the room getting darker as it approached. Shadows flitted in and out of the parlor where the technician ran the equipment. Suddenly, Tim began speaking for the ghost, stating the other spirits belonged to it, and demanding we go away.

As I argued with it, several others, including Diane Jones, saw a red face come through one of the holes in the ceiling, looking down at us. Jones began to panic and the temperature of the room dropped ten degrees. Spectators began to panic. Steven called for a break, due to the number of people in the room who were not experienced ghost hunters.

During the break, several of us went upstairs where Sherri and Theresa observed a shadow step out of a doorway at the end of the hall, silhouetted by the warning lights. It was the size and shape of an adult male. The shape dodged back into the room just as suddenly as it had appeared and disappeared before we got there.

It was after 11:00 P.M. Two members of the Sullivan Police Department, now off duty, arrived and asked if they could watch the rest of the investigation. This time, we got the odor of lilacs and then cigars and leather, all noticed by the new police witnesses as well as the investigators. Theresa could hear the sound of a piano, long since moved from the room. At that time, I took one of the officers upstairs, as Tim and I once again attempted to stir up the action.

Tim remained downstairs. The officer was using my still camera and Sherri was using a video recorder. I carried a digital voice recorder. About the same time, Tim and I began taunting the spirit, trapping the human-shaped shadow on an unused, decrepit stairway between floors.

With Tim below and myself above, it suddenly went through a wall into the next room. Tim chased it into the room, where it had disappeared. Tim mentioned that the batteries in his camera had died, and the Sullivan officer with me said our batteries had died also.

KLPW did one more EVP session, and this time we got moving shadows within the room, odors of leather and cigars, and knocks and thumps on the ceiling. When one of the investigators became physically ill, Steven stopped the investigation.

After KLPW left, we began another session in the dentist's room that involved Tim and me, Sherri, Theresa and Tim's daughter, as well as the Sullivan officers and their friends. I set up the video camera, and Sherri manned the still camera. I was taunting the spirit, when suddenly Sherri mentioned that the camera batteries had died again! Brand new batteries were placed in it not more than 15 minutes prior to this.

Later, checking the video taken during this time before the batteries drained. you could hear a sustained growling under my taunting. In the same timeframe, bits of plaster were being thrown at us from above, and bright orbs were photographed moving around us. In another room, once again, Tim's face was covered by a black mass.

A later check of evidence revealed golden glows from different sections of the mansion and the black masses.

Is the spirit that of a cantankerous, angry old general still prowling the halls of the mansion, frightening women and younger men with his fierce ways? A pianist—perhaps a graduate of Juilliard in New York, playing gently while the spirit of a cowardly young man hides among the wreckage of this once great mansion? The Harney Mansion is haunted, and the liveliest place of the dead at that end of Franklin County.

An idea, like a ghost, must be spoken to a little before it will explain itself.

—Charles Dickens

Photo by Dan Terry

Lyndee's, or Trooper Heaven, *as it was once known, located in Hermann, Missouri, may have unequalled police protection from the realm of the paranormal.*

Gasconade County, Missouri

Chapter 17

Trooper Heaven

for two police officers, death does not mean end of duty

He had broken into ten stores that night and had his entry down to a violent science. The burglar broke the small window with the back of the flashlight, reached in and turned the deadbolt from the inside. He went inside and straight to the cash register.

It was 11:30 P.M. The small town police were probably sitting at the station. The sidewalks had been rolled up nearly an hour and a half earlier. All was quiet; it was the time of the thief.

The thief couldn't open the register. He turned around and saw the prize: the green bank bag, zippered and full, sitting on the counter waiting for the morning deposit. Next to it, a careless waitress had left her tip money for the day, several bills and change, sitting on the bar.

Suddenly, he heard voices. Talking. Someone was here. The burglar did not consider the possible criminal charges that just tripled because someone was in the building, making it burglary in the first degree. This was Hermann, Missouri. Someone in there probably had a gun, and was not afraid to use it.

The smell of cigar smoke filled the room. Someone was coming closer. There was a loud noise, more talking. The burglar ran out of the store—empty handed. That night, this was the only business broken into that he did not get cash from. It was also the only store that had the money sitting in plain sight.

Lynn Helming, owner of Lyndee's restaurant in Hermann, often wondered why the thief left without the money. While he was never caught, locals believed they knew who he was. While he never spoke of the incident, one psychic from Illinois did, telling Lynn that the spirits in her restaurant were her "night watchmen, or security guards."

Founded in 1837 by the German Settlement Society of Philadelphia, the City of Hermann was designed to be a German Garden of Eden. They wanted a German settlement that could be self-sufficient and maintain the traditional native values and culture they had brought over from the Old World. After purchasing 11,300 acres of Gasconade River Valley land at a cost of $15,600, George Bayer was over-tasked with taking care of the settlers. The city was named for German hero Hermann der Cherusker, who helped defeat the Romans at the battle of Teutoburg Forest in the year 9 CE.

The steep, rocky ground made crops difficult, so the settlers, in their determination or stubborn will to succeed, began growing grapes and making wine. Today, Hermann and the surrounding area boasts seven wineries, and produces nearly a third of Missouri's wine.

In 1842, a steamboat named "Big Hatchie" blew up at the wharf in Hermann, killing some 70 people. Some died in the explosion, some burned, some drowned. Many bodies were never recovered, and at least 35 were buried in a mass grave at the city cemetery, where a monument to that tragic day yet stands.

Lyndee's restaurant began life under the ownership of Ralph Grannemann, who originally built the structure as a gas station on Highway 19 up the hill from the Highway 100 intersection. This was where cars that had been involved in traffic accidents all over Gasconade County were towed before being sent on. The station was then owned by a man named George, and was known as George's Service Station. Local legend suggests that George died there. Eventually, Ralph built a restaurant there and Harold Hildebrand owned the business. A former police officer, Harold ran the restaurant for two years, before becoming ill and retiring, selling the business. Harold ran his restaurant with an iron fist, making sure it was clean, and the service was fast. Harold put up with no monkey business.

During the 50's and 60's, these roads were long, dark and crooked, and that was where the police and highway patrol officers ate and socialized. The business was dubbed, "Trooper Heaven", and went by that nickname for years.

Lynn remembers fondly the days her restaurant was known as Trooper Heaven. Those days had passed, however, even before she purchased the business. Lynn has owned Lyndee's for 12 years, and has passed the management duties to her daughter, Kecia, although she still keeps a hand in it.

I was told about it by a local gas station employee in a neighboring town—a friend of Kecia's. One night, while visiting Kecia and her mother, the topic came up and he was told that the restaurant was haunted. After further discussion, in which he brought up the idea of contacting Spookstalker, they agreed and I was invited in.

On May 27, 2008, Sherri and I went to Lyndee's for an investigation. In addition to Kecia and Lynn, I had asked for the assistance of Tim Clifton and Steven LaChance. They had invited me on several hunts in the past, and everyone who knows Tim knows that if there is a ghost around, he will find it. Plus, after their many demonic cases, I thought they could use a Casper hunt.

Tim's daughter, Ginny, also came along. Ginny seems to have inherited her father's psychic abilities. We all went inside, and I interviewed Kecia and Lynn while the others walked around and began their psychic investigations.

For 12 years, Lynn had been ignoring the creepy feelings and hearing her name being called from an empty room. Many employees have quit working at the restaurant after seeing things. One waitress saw someone she did not recognize wearing a white shirt in the kitchen, seeing him through the service window. She ran around to check on who was in the kitchen, finding no one.

Regular customers have also caught a glimpse of the white-shirted man through the service window into the kitchen, but none have met him.

One day, several customers and employees watched as a photo on the wall, which had hung there for years, suddenly left the wall and fell, not straight down, but in a swooping, gliding motion, hitting the floor and sliding under a booth without breaking the glass or denting the frame. The photo was replaced, and employees attempted to make it fall again, without success.

During an evening shift, Lynn reported another waitress was working when she saw a chubby, curly-haired, freckled-faced boy of about ten standing in the aisle. She asked the child if he needed anything, but got no response. Meanwhile other customers stopped and watched her speaking.

When she asked again if he needed something, the child disappeared right before her eyes! Confused, Lynn looked around, realizing that the customers were watching her. She asked the nearest table if they saw where the child went. With a look of disbelief, the patrons said they had seen no child, but watched as she stood in the aisle and spoke to the air. No one else saw the boy, whom she had seen clearly and solidly standing in front of her. The waitress quit immediately, leaving the restaurant at that moment forever.

Kecia mentioned an evening when she had been there after hours with some friends after the bars closed. They were having a last beer when a glass lifted up from the shelf below the counter, moved around the corner and shattered on the floor. The party was over. Kecia said she believed the spirit was watching over the restaurant, and wanted her and her friends out. Interestingly, one of the subjects with her that night, someone she had just met, was arrested for severely beating his girlfriend a few days later.

Tim returned to the counter where we sat. He informed me that he had walked into the dining room, where most of the activity seemed to have occurred. There he saw a man with a mustache and white shirt, but he had stepped into the wall and disappeared. Tall and thin, Lynn said that described Harold Hildebrand.

We set up the cameras. I placed my video camera in the corner near a china hutch then we went inside the dining room and began an EVP session. I used the K2 meter looking for EMF spikes while Sherri took still photographs as Steven and Tim attempted to make contact.

During the first attempt, both Ginny and I observed a black orb cross the ceiling above us. There were also some sprites, or flashes of light, over in the corner. I went over there, and Ginny believed something left as I approached. Tim said I had annoyed a spirit by standing in what it believed to be its space.

Tim and Steven both believed they had made contact with an adult male. Because of the history and demographics of Hermann, Tim attempted to speak German, having prepared some questions in German in advance.

Suddenly, Steven burst into laughter. The atmosphere seemed to lighten in the room, and even Tim smiled. Steven said he had gotten the impression that the spirit thought Tim was funny, and was laughing at his attempts to speak German. Steven believed the spirit was proud of being an American, and was taking Tim's attempts to contact him in the old language as a joke.

We started again. Tim believed a ghost of a child was in the room. Steven and Ginny agreed. Tim pointed at a corner of the room, and I approached with the K2 meter. Ginny and Steven both said the spirit was cringing, afraid of the two large men approaching him with strange objects in their hand.

Tim and I sat down while Steven and Tim attempted to make contact. Steven believed the child had been killed in an accident, and was in the vehicle when it was towed to the station in the days when this was George's garage. He was afraid to go to the light, and had waited here instead for all these years.

During this time I watched as the light beyond the folding door, a door that separated this dining room from the main part of the restaurant, began flickering as if something was moving around inside. After a few moments' break, I set up the camera again and informed the group I would be stepping into the restaurant as they began again to contact the child or adult spirits.

Inside the restaurant, I thought I saw a shadow person walk quickly into the kitchen. Finding no one in there, I continued photographing the area. After some time, I began walking back to the dining room. As I approached the door, I heard a bang, which sounded like a heavy glass salt or pepper shaker being slammed down on the table. I ran back to the other side of the restaurant but found nothing out of place.

I returned slowly to the door. To the right of the door was a small room separated by the trendy western-style saloon doors, beyond which were the two doors to the restrooms. As I walked to the door to return to the group, I heard what sounded like fingernails scratching down the wall on the other side of the swinging doors. At the exact moment the noise ended, I heard Steven on the other side of the door ask for the spirit to make a noise for them. As so often happened, since time seems to mean nothing to the other side, the question was answered before it was even asked.

I asked if anyone else had heard that noise, and all of them had. I returned to the dining room, as Tim made contact with a spirit.

At first, Tim thought he was speaking with one of the spirits who had something do to with the restaurant or garage. He began feeling pain in the chest and said he was having trouble breathing. He felt hot water falling on him, maybe a summer rain. More trouble breathing. We discussed heart attacks, congestive heart failure and pneumonia, all of which can cause someone to drown in their own bodily fluids. Tim knew it was a very painful death. It began to affect Tim, and Steven asked me to turn on the lights and help Tim break the contact. A break was called.

After a rest, all of the women returned to the dining room in an effort to make contact with the child, who appeared to be afraid of men. Steven, Tim and I stayed in the restaurant, where I remembered the story of the Big Hatchie. Tim realized that this was what he had been feeling—the drowning, the hot rain as the boiler exploded, sending hot water up and around like rain. The cemetery that held the unclaimed and unidentified bodies was less than a block behind this store, and the waterfront was only a few blocks away in the other direction.

Could a wandering spirit, traveling from the place where his body lay in a mass grave to the scene of his death, have been attracted to Tim's medium abilities, and seen a chance to get his story out? Some, including myself, believe that for lost souls, the other side is a darkness filled with spirits that have no place to go, refusing or afraid to move to the final judgment. To those wandering souls, some living people with certain psychic abilities seem like a lighthouse to a storm-tossed sailor. They head for the light of that person, looking for help or security. With some children, similar to the movie "The Sixth Sense", which was loosely based on a real person, the souls were seeking their help because the children could see them. This could drive the poor kid, and his family, to question their sanity. Tim, on the other hand, understands what is happening but often is unable to break the connection himself, relying on his friends to help break it for him.

Soon, it was time for all of us to start again. Ginny believed she made contact with the child, who said he enjoyed playing with the checkers and toys that Lynn left out for children. The cameras were set up, and the lights turned down again.

Steven began the last EVP session. The atmosphere of the room had again changed, seemingly darker inside. Again, as Steven spoke, I could see movement in the darkness, near the door. The small, green light on the back of my digital video recorder, shining brightly in the dark against the china hutch in the background, seemed to be blinking. As I watched, something continued to cross between the camera and the hutch, causing the light reflected on the hutch to appear to flash.

The session continued. Suddenly, Steven stopped speaking. There was a long pause, broken when Steven said "Ok, this is going to sound really strange, but . . . "

Another long pause. "I can't believe I am going to say this," Another pause. "You are going to think I'm crazy, I can't believe this."

"Steve," I said. "Just say it!"

"Law Enforcement. I am seeing a cop. Police." Ginny concurred, saying "I knew you were going to say that." Lynn mentioned that Harold had been a police officer for the City of Hermann. Steven replied that this was someone else.

The activity got stronger. Steven asked what cologne Tim was wearing. He replied none. He then asked what I had on. Because spirits often use odors to make their presence known, I never wear cologne or anything with a strong smell on an investigation. I answered that I was not wearing a scent. Steven swore he could smell Old Spice aftershave. Tim also said he could smell something, but could not identify it except to say he had smelled it before.

Surprisingly, a very strong odor of tobacco, specifically cherry pipe tobacco, seemed to blanket my face. While I felt no wind or air, the odor was so strong it was as if someone blew smoke directly into my face. I informed the group that the odor was around me, and I knew what it was because my father smoked the same type of tobacco.

Tim agreed. That's what he had been smelling as well. The odor faded around me but got stronger around Kecia. Then Tim and Steven, who were sitting right across from each other, got it as well.

"There is another cop in here," Steven said. "And I'm getting a name . . . Harry?"

The odor of cigar smoke returned to me, and then to Kecia and back to me. Steven believed there was a reason it seemed to stay close to me. I mentioned a former deputy sheriff of Gasconade County named Harry Chisum, who had been running for sheriff when he died in a tractor accident in the late 1990's. But Lynn had another idea.

"Back when Harold was here, there was a county sheriff named Harry Heberle. They hung out here back when I was a little girl. All the troopers and officers hung out here. In fact, they use to call this place Trooper Heaven!"

The room exploded in a flurry of activity. The green camera light reflecting on the hutch began flashing, as if a spirit was doing jumping jacks between the camera and wall. Tim and Steven started laughing simultaneously, and the odor of cherry pipe tobacco seemed to be running from Kecia to me, and back again. Dark orbs flew over our heads, and the ambient light in the room got brighter. The spirits were happy!

Steven sighed, still smiling. "Dan, this is why you are here. Think about it, someone meets Kecia, and they talk about ghosts. He works in the same town you work in. He came to you. This is too much coincidence. They wanted you here!"

We ended the investigation that night. The owner and her daughter were delighted to know that the officers were staying and protecting the restaurant. Lynn suddenly remembered the night a few years ago, when someone broke into the restaurant on a night when ten other businesses had been broken into. Even though tip money was sitting on the bar, along with the bank deposit, the restaurant was the only place where cash had not been taken. Did her ghosts, referred to by one psychic as her night watchmen, prevent the crime? Lynn believes so.

Lynn is planning to create a shadow box in honor of law enforcement, and place it over one booth to give her spirits, still serving and protecting even in death, a table to call their own. For these blue knights, Trooper Heaven is close enough for them.

The spirit of the dead who stood in life before these are again in death around thee, and their will shall overshadow thee; be still.

—Edgar Allan Poe

Photo by Dan Terry

Cannon at Bloody Hill *on Wilson's Creek Battlefield near Springfield.*

Greene County, Missouri

Chapter 18

There'll Be Fightin' Like Hell in Ten Minutes

at Wilson's Creek Battlefield, the war may be over, but some of the soldiers have yet to be relieved

John Ray, local postmaster and owner of the cornfield across the valley, sat on his porch watching as his three children took the family horses to the spring house. For the last couple of days, he had watched from this porch as soldiers, first Union, then Confederate, crawled across the cornfield, damaging the crops he depended on to get through the winter. Concerned that the armies may try to 'liberate' his horses, he kept a close eye on the kids.

Soon, a lone figure in a blue uniform rode up to the children.

Ray watched as the mounted soldier leaned down and spoke with the children, then rode away. The three kids, along with the horses, came quickly back to the house.

"Dad, we'd better get out of here," John Ray's son told him. "That officer said there'd be fightin' like Hell in less than ten minutes!"

From the vantage point on his porch, John could see the two armies slowly converge. Too late for escape, he called to his wife, Roxanne, to go to the small basement, taking the children, their loyal slave, Aunt Rhoda, her children, and the hired hand, Julius Short. John shut the basement door and returned to the porch to watch the battle.

Some 5400 blue-clad troops were meeting across the valley with 11,600 Confederate troops. General Nathaniel Lyon, former commander of the St. Louis Garrison, knew his troops were badly outnumbered but hoped the surprise of an early morning attack would turn the tide early. The Confederates were mostly the Missouri State Guard, a group of undisciplined, barely trained Missouri farm boys with no experience, but they were strong in number.

It was August 10, 1861.

At 5:00 A.M., the battle started. At first, the plan worked. The inexperienced Missouri State Guard began to retreat. By 6:00 A.M., the Union forces were pushing back the boys in gray.

But Gen. Lyon had underestimated the Boys from Missouri and their leadership. By 6:30 A.M., the Confederates rallied and their artillery opened up on the Union forces occupying the high land, forever after known as "Bloody Hill." Soon, the smaller Union forces were holding on by their teeth, as wave after wave of Confederate troops attacked. General Lyon had been wounded twice, and had one horse shot out from under him. Another officer gave him his own horse, and Lyon told him he feared the day was lost.

Returning to battle, Lyon was seen waving his hat as he attempted to rally members of the 2nd Kansas and the Iowa armies to fight. From a thicket of brush, a series of shots rang out and a ball struck General Lyon in the left chest.

Lyon looked down at his bleeding wound, then slowly dismounted as the Iowa forces fought back, driving the troops from the thicket and back down the hill. As he reached the ground, his legs gave out and he fell into the arms of his aide, saying "Lehmen, I am killed." After the death of their commander, a retreat was ordered. The Southern cause had won the day.

After the first few shots at the John Ray home, Confederate surgeons raised a yellow flag over the house, signifying it as a field hospital. No more rounds were fired at the house and both sides used it for the dead and dying. The body of Gen. Lyon was left under a black oak tree nearby.

During the retreat, his body was forgotten and was retrieved by the Confederates who, under orders of General Price, took it to the field hospital.

After hours of clinging to each other in the dark basement as the sounds of battle and the moans of the dying assaulted their ears, the family of John Ray came up from below to a vision of Hell. On the table, last seen set for a large, country breakfast, a soldier was screaming as his leg was being cut off without the assistance of anesthesia. The plates and silverware, so recently set neatly on the table, were dumped against the wall.

The family immediately began to assist in the care of the wounded soldiers. The house was filled with sounds of the screaming and moaning of the dying men as the family brought water and attempted to comfort them.

Temporary shelters were hastily erected in the yard to keep the sun off the men. As the porch and rooms of the small cabin filled with the wounded, the blue and gray clothing had turned to a uniform bloody red.

The body of General Lyon was brought in and examined. Then Union troops, under a flag of truce, were allowed in to pick up the body and transfer it to Springfield. It was temporarily buried there on the land belonging to the Missouri Governor Claiborne Fox Jackson until arrangements could be made to transport the General to Connecticut, where he was later buried with full military honors.

Later, the Congress of the United States would vote a congressional Thanks to Lyon, whose sacrifice rallied the pro-Union people of Missouri and helped prevent the state from being forced to officially support the Southern cause.

The Battle of Wilson's Creek, or Battle of Oak Hills as the

Confederates called it, resulted in 1235 Union men killed, wounded or missing, and 1184 Confederate killed or wounded.

According to the guides at the Wilson's Creek battlefield park, the bodies were gathered, Union and Confederate, and placed in a sink hole on Bloody Hill, then covered with dirt. Some time later, the bodies were removed and replaced in the National Cemetery in Springfield.

In his book "Haunted Ozark Battlefields", author and Civil war Historian Steve Cottrell discussed the Wilson Creek Battlefield. One year, according to Cottrell, reenactors, or people who dress up in period costume and recreate historical events, were preparing for a reenactment of the Battle of Wilson's Creek. During the dark time just before sunrise, Union infantry reenactors on a march noticed a solitary figure following them on horseback, wearing a Civil War uniform. At first, they thought it was a member of another unit of reenactors, possibly Cavalry. Eventually, the ghostly horseman disappeared.

Later, they checked with the cavalry units and discovered that none of them had their horses out or were even awake yet at that time of day. One last spirit soldier, or perhaps General Lyon, inspecting the troops?

John Harris is the founder and lead investigator for Springfield Paranormal Research. He started his research group with his family in 2000, investigating all over the nation. In 2005, John expanded the team to include other investigators. Today, Springfield Paranormal Research has nine full investigators and most of them got their start at the Wilson's Creek Battlefield.

"Something happens to me each time I go out there," John said. "The first time, as I came down the ramp in the wheelchair from my van, I was grabbed by the front of the shirt and jerked out of the chair onto the ground. I was helped back into the chair, and the side of my shirt where I had been grabbed was ripped. Under that, there were three scratches on my chest."

John went on to say that each time he goes out, something often pulls on him, and he almost always ends up with scratch marks. "Now, the investigators photograph me before we leave, and follow me with the digital recorders and cameras. Recently, I was again pulled out of the chair, and when I was helped back in, there were scratches that weren't on my chest before."

John doesn't know who or what is doing this, or why. He did say he doesn't really believe it's against him personally, but theorizes that the spirits have never seen an electric wheelchair before, and don't understand it.

His team has heard EVP's of gunshots, which John disregards because of the closeness of farms to the park. But one evening he and his team heard something he can't shrug off so easily.

"We all heard drums being played, very plainly." John reported.

"It sounded like a march. But, when we tried to hear it later on the recording, the noise of the crickets was too loud."

On their first trip, Springfield Paranormal Research took a photo of one of the investigators as she walked down a path. When it was checked, there was an image, in a very light gray mist-like substance, of what appears to be a full size horse with a rider. On the second investigation, which was on December 31, 2004, a photo was taken of Bloody Hill. Between trees, there seemed to be a solitary figure standing. As it was enlarged, the figure appeared to be a blue-cloaked military man with a beard. As I looked at the enlargement, I asked John a question:

"Is it just me, or does that appear to be General Lyon?"

"Before I changed my web site," John Harris answered, "I had a portrait of General Lyon next to that photo. I believe it looks just like him!"

General Lyon was described as a slight built man, dressed somewhat shabbily, with a beard. The figure on the hill does resemble the portraits of the general at the visitors center.

John and his team went there to investigate on the anniversary of the battle. "There is an eerie feeling to the place on the anniversary of the fight," John said, "that wasn't there days or weeks before."

Most of their personal experiences happened on Bloody Hill. While John is skeptical when it comes to psychics, he once was there with a psychic, who began feeling "exploding in the chest" and shortness of breath, as if drowning. During another investigation the temperature suddenly dropped 28 degrees, from 55 down to 27 degrees. This was near two cannons sitting down at the bottom of Bloody Hill.

During another investigation, investigators noticed the odor of

Photo by John Harris

Could it be *that this photo, which appears to reveal a lone soldier in the distance, is actually General Lyon, revisiting the scene of his death?*

something dead on Bloody Hill. They separated and searched the area in a wide circle, over 100 yards in diameter, looking for a dead animal that could be making that odor. Finding nothing, the only other possibility was that they were near the sinkhole where the bodies of the fallen soldiers had been placed before they were moved to the National Cemetery.

In the opinion of John Harris, the battlefield at Wilson's Creek is haunted. Does General Lyon still command over a ghostly army of the dead? Or did the horrors of such intense, close-quarter battle somehow imprint itself on the very atmosphere at Bloody Hill? Men on both sides fought bravely and died with honor for their respective sides in the hot, sticky field one humid day in August.

They've earned their rest.

Sorry, Venkman, I'm terrified beyond the capacity for rational thought.

—Ghostbusters, 1984

Photo Courtesy of Stephen Bine

When the baby is giggling at nothing *or the dog is staring at the empty corner of the house, ignore it. It's probably nothing. . . .*

Various Missouri Locations

Chapter 19

Livin' With the Dead

i leave them alone, they leave me alone

I've heard this phrase more and more when talking to people who live in haunted houses. It seems that people who live with ghosts get used to them like getting used to a dripping faucet or a creaky step. Or maybe, more like the adult children who moved away to college, but returned to live with mom and dad until they got on their feet. Not so much a problem as an annoyance. Something you just get used to.

True demonic cases are fairly rare compared to ghostly haunting. You hear more about the demonic type because they become more dramatic and make interesting screenplays. By far, the most common haunting seems to be quiet movement and the occasional sound or smell. Many people who live with such spirits don't talk about it or learn to ignore it.

When investigating and researching for my first book, I ran across Frances and Betsy Vollertson. I had known both of them for years, but had no idea they lived in a haunted house until I was researching for the first book.

In 1971, Frances and her husband moved into the old farmhouse with their daughter, Betsy, and a son. The previous owners, an older couple, had both passed on. Betsy knew the wife had died some time in the 60's, and their son would come from St. Louis and tend to the yard and house.

The first spring, Frances recalls, she was lying in bed one warm evening and heard music. She remembered it was old-time music, even for the early 70's. At first, she thought it came from the direction of the nearby creek. She checked the window and slowly came to the realization that the music was coming from a closet in the bedroom. Finding nothing, she returned to bed and tried to ignore the music. It was many years later that her husband, Jim, admitted to also hearing the music. Afraid of being thought of as crazy, he never told anyone.

Over the years, the activity came and went. Frances and Betsy both reported the odor of pipe tobacco, even after Jim stopped smoking cigarettes. No one in the house ever smoked a pipe or cigar. Frances could even identify the brand—Captain Black.

The spirits were never mean or angry. In fact, one was somewhat motherly. Many times, often several times a month, Frances was tucked into bed. She said she could even see as the blankets were shoved in around her. Eventually, she would ask the spirit to stop and leave her alone. It always would.

Unfortunately, the same could not be said of the family dogs. They were teased or aggravated each night, never getting a night's sleep. When I interviewed Betsy and her mother, it had been less than two weeks since moving into their new home within the city limits of New Haven. In the days before moving, the dogs were constantly barking and yelping in the night. Since the move, neither dog has failed to sleep quietly all night.

Neither Betsy nor Frances knows who the spirits are. Once, a Ouija® board was brought in by a family member. It indicated that the house had been built on an Indian burial ground. According to the board, there were three ghosts in the house, a white male, his American Indian wife, and their child. Interestingly, during the rebuilding of a bridge nearby, the construction company did uncover evidence of a burial area.

A check by a university geological group indicated it was the burial area of one person only at that time, and construction continued. Perhaps there were more buried in the area.

Betsy remembered once getting up in the night and being led down the stairs by a white human-size mist. I asked her if she was afraid.

"No. I never felt fear. Remember, I moved in there as a little girl," Betsy said. "I grew up with these, and they never hurt anyone. I just went into the kitchen and got my milk and cookies."

Frances also dealt with the white mist. "I was alone in the house, taking a bath," Betsy recalled. "One of the dogs was sitting at the door, which was open because I was the only one there. I looked up, and saw a white mist floating down the stairway."

The other things were not unusual for a haunted home. They heard their names being called from empty rooms, sounds of things falling with nothing out of place, and hearing the front door open, later finding it closed. Betsy's father and brother never mentioned the ghost and, for a time, she thought that only she and her mother heard it. Recently, while she talked to her brother about it, he made the statement, "I grew up there. I know what it's like."

Betsy and Frances both believe it was just the ghosts having fun. Or, as Betsy says, "They're just entertaining themselves."

As we talked, I got the impression that neither thought the ghost followed them to the new house. Betsy believes that one of the ghosts did follow her to the trailer she moved into for a short time some years ago. While they don't mind the spirits, they are glad the dogs are sleeping through the night.

Then, Betsy mentioned hearing the music. I asked if she thought the radio was turning itself on, and she replied no, that she had just heard music coming from nowhere. When I reminded them that this was how it started in the first place some 37 years ago, the two women looked at each other with surprise. Neither had thought of it.

Pauline Stout has a different story. Pauline spent a large part of the 1960's living in a house on Beethoven Street just off of Morganford in St. Louis. A large, old home, she had no problems until she brought in the bad spirits.

"I worked for the post office," Pauline told me. "Several of us would get together at my house, and have a séance or play with the Ouija® board. One night, we had a séance, and after my friends left, I went to bed. A decorative birdcage I kept flowers in, which was bolted to the brick wall, suddenly flew off the wall and crashed into the wall on the other side of the room."

Later that night, the sounds of chains being dragged across the ceiling kept them up all night. After that, a black mass was seen all over the house, including looking over her daughter as she slept in her bed one night. Pauline also reported that one step was creaky, and as she walked down the stairs, even though she was past the step, it would creak as if someone was coming down behind her. Unlike Betsy and Frances, however, this spirit was less than protective.

Later, one of her co-workers told her that they "forgot to close the door" they had opened with the séance. There continued to be strange noises, and the bathroom door would open by itself. Eventually, Pauline and her family would leave that house. However, she keeps tabs on the house, and has noticed that several families have moved in and out of the house recently, sometimes rather quickly.

A few weeks before I spoke to Pauline, she had walked around the building and a neighbor walked over to see if they were interested in buying it. When Pauline explained that she used to live there and why they had left, the neighbor shared with them her own ghost stories of her house and others in the block. Pauline wondered if it was the area that was haunted, or if she had unleashed some of the hell those folks are living with.

Two years after his grandpa died, Stephen Bine purchased the old hunting cabin his grandfather loved so much. Stephen's dad inherited the old cabin, rebuilt it into a home, and then sold it to his son.

Stephen's idea that something else was in the old cabin started slowly as most ghost adventures do. The baby giggled at nothing, the dogs would stare at one spot. There were even cold spots in the house.

Stephen's grandfather, Steve, was a very faithful Catholic. Steve had been very active in church his entire life. He and two friends, who passed away before Steve, used the cabin as a retreat almost every weekend for years. They went up together, as retired friends, to mow and clean the cabin. Only church came before his time at the beloved cabin in the woods.

Stephen didn't consider the idea of ghosts—at least not at first.

"Each night," Stephen related, "My wife would set the clock radio to go off at 6:00 A.M. She always set the radio on WIL-FM, a local country radio station. That way, we would wake up to country music."

"Almost every morning, at 6:00 A.M., the radio would turn on and it would be playing a religious station. Not gospel music, but I guess you'd call it an evangelical station. Sermons! This was almost constant." That's when the idea of his grandpa's ghost first occurred to him.

Weekly at least, sometimes more, the radio station would be moved across the dial. Not just another station coming in closely, but halfway across the dial!

But the proof came with a photograph of the living room. It clearly shows the dog staring at the wall, and a large, white mist forming there. On the sofa are two more white mists as if they were sitting on the cushions. Were grandpa and his hunting friends there? Stephen has no doubt.

In my ghost adventures, I've met many people who live with paranormal experiences as a daily occurrence. Others live with demonic or evil activity. There is a big difference between the two, but for regular human spirits intent on living their own after-life lives, if you can live with the occasional radio change or glimpses of someone walking by, they'll usually leave you alone.

And, you'll have a story to tell on one of those dark and stormy nights. . . .

Photo by Dan Terry

Sometimes when the night is quiet and you thought all was well,
but have an uneasy feeling, it may be because
someone or something is watching you.

Chapter 20

Conclusion

the end may only be the beginning

And so, we bring this book of adventures to a close. I've taken you from haunted hotels to spooky jails, from ghostly battlefields and demonic truck stops to possessed bridges and angelic hideaways, from the happy halls of a supernatural school to the friendly police ghosts of Lyndee's, to angry Civil War generals and spiritually-possessed skulls stalking the halls of a museum. And yet, we have no clear answers.

I have no answers for you. I recently read that there are some 20,000 amateur ghost-hunting groups active in the United States. I've seen many come and go. The evidence is mounting, yet the non-believers will continue to deny the truth.

Ghost hunting is not for everyone. Many would feel safer reading about it from the safety of their homes, lighted by electricity and secure from the horrors of the lantern-lit nights of the days of yore. However, I have discovered that ghosts are everywhere! Most of them want only to go on with their ghostly business, moving around you in the daylight world quietly and unseen. Only a very few like to be seen or heard.

When the baby is giggling at nothing or the dog is staring at the empty corner of the house, ignore it. It's probably nothing......

Sleep Well.

—Dan Terry, "Spookstalker"

Acknowledgements

There are just too many people to thank, so if I have forgotten someone, I apologize.

Steven Lachance, Greg Myers, and Tim Clifton, have all taught me a lot about ghost hunting and I appreciate their help and trust.

My wife, Sherri, has been by my side for most of the ghost hunts and is, indeed, braver than I am.

Of course, Darren McGavin's portrayal of Carl Kolchak in the Night Stalker series started me on this long, strange trip.

A lot of people thought I should write the first book, *Beyond the Shadows*, but only my publisher, Sue Blesi, put her money where her mouth was and published it for me. Her belief in me is gratefully acknowledged.

Two members of my team, Loretta Coffman and Jamie Eckerle, did great work and helped me a lot before they formed their own team, Missouri State Paranormal Investigations. Also, I appreciate the brainstorming sessions shared with Officer Meg Parks.

A special thanks to the Friends of Historic Booneville, for their assistance with the stories at the Cooper County jail.

Also, the folks at the Saint Charles County Historic Society went out of the way to be helpful, and gave me information I didn't even know I needed.

The following is a list of web sites for places and people to whom I owe a debt of gratitude for the contents of this book.

Steven Lachance:	www.stevenalachance.com
Greg Myers, PTF	www.paranormaltaskforce.com
MSPI	www.missouristateparanormalinvestigators.com
The Parlor Bed and Breakfast	www.theparlorbandb.com
Prosperity School B and B	www.prosperitybandb.com
Dr. Michael Henry	www.stcharlesghosts.com
Independence Jail	www.jchs.com
Betsy Belanger, Lemp Mansion Tours	www.stlspiritsearch.com
Nick Corey	www.jasperhaunts.com
Springfield Paranormal	www.springfieldparanormal.net
Garden House Bed and Breakfast	www.gardenhousebedandbreakfast.com
Garth Mansion Bed and Breakfast	www.garthmansion.com
Cooper County Jail: Friends of Historic Booneville	www.mo-river.net/history/cooper
Harney Mansion	The Harney Mansion Foundation PO Box 398 Sullivan, MO 63080

Order Form

Mail to: Missouri Kid Press
Post Office Box 111
Stanton, Missouri 63079

or

email: missourikidpress@hotmail.com

Price Per Copy: $ 14.99*
Shipping Per Copy: 4.00*

*Note: Price and Shipping Subject to Change

Name ______________________________

Street ______________________________

City / State / Zip ______________________________

Telephone / Email Address ______________________________

It is not necessary to remove this form from the book to place an order. Please verify current price with publisher prior to ordering. NOTE: Special pricing and shipping reduction available for 12 or more copies to one address. Contact publisher for specifics.